LIVING INSYNC™

LIVING INSYNC™

Creating Your Life with Balance and Purpose

Susan Pilgrim, Ph.D.

Health Communications, Inc.
Deerfield Beach, Florida

Library of Congress Cataloging-in-Publication Data

Pilgrim, Susan (date)
    Living InSync: creating your life with balance and purpose/
    Susan Pilgrim.
    p. cm.
    Includes bibliographical references.
    ISBN 1-55874-340-5 (pbk.)
    1. Self-actualization (Psychology) 2. Self-actualization (Psychology)—
Problems, exercises, etc. 3. Mind and body. 4. Mind and body—Problems,
exercises, etc. 5. New Thought. I. Title.
BF637.S4P54 1995
158'.1—dc20   95-8200
                                                                CIP

Publisher: Health Communications, Inc.
               3201 S.W. 15th Street
               Deerfield Beach, Florida 33442-8190

Cover design by Lawna P. Oldfield

To each person
who believes in my work
and in me.

Out of the blackness of the seemingly endless dark,
comes the light—a bright white light
sparkling faintly in the distance.
See the light.
Focus on the light.
The light is God.
The light is your soul.
The light is your essence.
The light is your feeling of peace.
The light is your guide.
The light is always with you.
You are the light.

Susan Pilgrim, Ph.D.
Excerpted from *The Seashore Collection*
© 1991 by Life Investments, Atlanta, Georgia

PREFACE

What began as a routine full-body massage on a Friday afternoon several years ago, became the catalyst for the powerful changes that were to occur in my life. I responded to the expert massaging techniques used by the therapist with uncontrollable wailing and sobbing. I decided this uncharacteristic and unexpected response was something that could not be ignored. I felt compelled to find out what was going on within me. This was the beginning of my own journey of self-discovery and the foundation for the work I do today.

The following Monday I made an appointment with a clinical psychologist. My educational background and the work I'd been doing for a number of years made me skeptical. I was very familiar with the counseling process and had served in a counseling capacity myself. I had only sought out such assistance once before when I was in college, and that experience left a lot to be desired. Despite my skepticism, I knew this experience was beyond my ability to cope with alone. I couldn't understand it.

I recounted the superficial details of the story of my life to the therapist and laughed at the parts that I had no other way of dealing with. I related the incidents when my mother chased me around the kitchen with a yardstick while I yelled loud enough for the neighbors to hear, "Please, Momma, please don't kill me!" I recounted these situations with inappropriate laughter, particularly the one when the yardstick broke in three pieces. The therapist looked sternly at me and said, "Susan, that's not funny." And she was right—it had been the only way I could deal with the pain that came from knowing that the woman who gave me birth and was supposed to love me was out to harm me.

And so I began the work, the excruciatingly slow, painful and dark process to uncover my past while attempting to make sense out of my life as a child. Those were dark times; those were critical times. Without revisiting, uncovering, and reckoning with my past, my gifts could not be used to their fullest extent. The incidents of physical, sexual and, most especially, emotional abuse and neglect are far too many to be recounted here, but some typical incidents will show what my life was like during the formative years. What happened to me during that time had a devastating effect on the first fifteen years of my adult life.

When I was born, my mother was sick. My father was gone. She asked the minister if he and his wife would take care of me for a few days until she could get back on her feet. The minister and his wife agreed. I lived with them for the next four years or so. When they moved to another state, my mother asked if they would take me with them. They had grown to love me and agreed. My mother would visit me periodically. From what I can recall, those visits were strained. I knew she was my mother, but I couldn't understand the relationship. When one of the minister's relatives became ill in another state, the minister called my mother and asked if she could keep me while they went to see him. My mother agreed. On returning from the trip, they called my mother to let her know they'd be by to pick me up. My mother told them not to bother because she had made arrangements to keep me. Nothing was explained to me at the time. I was very confused. I immediately began to miss the love I had felt from these people who had taken such good care of me for the first few years of my life.

I began living with my mother in the mountains of North Carolina. I was five years old. She worked with a church mission. We had strict rules about how, when and where we were supposed to do things. When the dinner bell was rung, we had to report to the dining room. If we were late, we had to go to bed without supper. This rule was to teach us to be on time. There was no flexibility. Whenever I was late for dinner, I would be spanked before I was sent to bed because I was embarrassing my mother by not following the rules. She would tell me if she lost her job, it would be my fault. That's a heavy burden for a five-year-old to carry.

One afternoon I went to visit some friends who lived up the path from us. A terrible storm with lightening, thunder and much rain came up. I had to leave so I could be back in time for supper. My friends told me I couldn't go because it was too dangerous. I begged them to let me leave because I knew I would be in so much trouble if I were late again. Many times I'd been to bed without supper. I didn't have an adult sense of time.

Finally I ran out of their house, running as fast as I could through the storm, and eventually ran into my mother who was looking for me. She had a long switch in her hand and began to beat my legs when I got within her reach. Blood began pouring from the opened skin. The switch was from a thorn bush. My mother beat me and yelled at me until we got back to the house. After she cleaned the wounds, she made me swear never to tell anyone. I, of course, was sent to bed without supper. I'd like to think she didn't know about the thorns on the switch, but she never told me so.

When I was 11, my mother had a boyfriend who would spend the night. He had a gun. Since my mother and I slept in the same bed, so did the boyfriend. He slept between me and my mother. At night he would force me to use my hands to fondle his genitals. I was terrified. I was afraid if I didn't do what he wanted me to do that he would shoot my mother and me. I would be sick to my stomach but afraid to move, afraid to get out of bed until it was morning. My mother knew. It was a very small bed. She never said anything to him that I'm aware of. Eventually he went away. My mother never talked to me about what happened. I felt dirty and overwhelmingly ashamed. My sense of self worth, my feelings about healthy sexuality and my relationships were all damaged. I had grown to hate my mother.

I felt guilty since you're supposed to love your mother just because she is your mother.

As a teenager, I use to write my thoughts and feelings in a diary. I believed that a diary was your personal property, that other people would respect it and not read it. One day I came home from school and my mother was waiting for me. She began berating me for how I felt about her and for wanting to live with someone else. In a typical teenage style, I told her I didn't know what she was talking about. She slapped me across the face and said emphatically, "Yes, you do know what I'm talking about!" Then she pulled out my opened diary. All of my hopes, dreams and feelings were exposed to the very person that denied me what I really needed. I was devastated. I felt naked, ashamed and angry. From that point on, I shut down emotionally and refused to express my feelings and thoughts on paper.

Shortly after completing college, I began working in special education programs for a local school system. I became interested in helping kids who had difficulty learning and dealing with their behavior and emotions. I decided I would give these youngsters my time, energy and resources, often to the detriment of my own needs. Many of them suffered from emotional and physical abuse and neglect. Many were victims of sexual abuse. What was going on in their lives was unfair, traumatic and sad. My past paled in comparison with their present. I was the great minimizer; minimizing my own situation so I could shift my efforts to help them. I found that I had a positive influence on their lives. I held to the belief that if I could make a difference in their lives then they wouldn't have to suffer like I did.

I share these stories with you so you can understand that no matter what has happened, you can overcome the powerful hold that incidents and people from your past have held over you. You're not responsible for what happened as a child. You are responsible for how you deal with your past and, most importantly, how you deal with your present and future.

Perhaps these excerpts from my life give you an idea of how my life unfolded before I began making conscious choices to get what I want; before I began taking appropriate responsibility for my actions, feelings, thoughts and ideas.

In 1989, with the purpose of having a positive influence on the lives of those people with whom I come in contact, I started my company, Life Investments. Who would have ever thought that the newborn child abandoned by her biological mother for five years would emerge as a professional speaker, workshop facilitator, personal coach and writer? Who would have ever believed that I had a gift that was only being partially used, a gift that could positively impact the lives of others?

My life path has been difficult. The road has had many curves in many directions. There would be no blame if I'd taken the easy way out, blaming what happened—the abuse, neglect and disrespect—for the condition of my life and not bothering to change it. Yet, I chose the most difficult, the most challenging of all paths, the one of inner knowing, becoming fully aware of my responsibility to pursue what I want in life. The messages in this book are for you who have recognized the value of dealing with your "inner child" wounds and who are now ready to take responsibility for your life. It is for those who want to make conscious choices about what they want and for those who want to pursue with vigor the goals they set for themselves.

You'll find that the content and exercises are a reflection of and embedded in the beliefs of the practical philosophy of living InSync:

- We are unique and of worth.
- We deserve to be treated with dignity and respect.
- Our humanness is to be celebrated.
- We are complicated entities with a multidimensional essence of spirit, emotion, body, mind and human connections.
- Balance in all areas of our lives leads to purpose, fulfillment and harmony.

- Nurturing each of the five interconnected dimensions of life is essential.
- We have the power within us to do whatever we choose.
- We have the ability to take *gentle* control of our lives by making conscious choices.
- We must move out of our "comfort zones" in order to experience life.
- We must find our own way since there is no one *right* way.
- We can be our best without detracting from another's best.
- Our individual growth affects our professional productivity and that of the organization.

This book is about celebrating your life and sharing the gifts you've been given. This book reminds us that life, success, happiness and living InSync are *processes* requiring our time, energy, resources, perseverance and patience. The In Sync philosophy is one that I developed so I could make sense out of life and establish a firm foundation for my work. It's here for you to use until you've developed your own.

I spent many years being in the dark; it was how I survived. I experienced pain and emotional suffering to come out of the darkness. I wanted to do more than just survive. Now I revel in the light of life and love. The light's shining on me. It shines on you, too. Take the challenge and find out for your self.

In Life,

Susan Pilgrim, Ph.D.
Atlanta, Georgia
August 27, 1992

ACKNOWLEDGMENTS

My deep gratitude goes to the many people who have touched my life and have allowed me to touch theirs. I honor my healers and teachers, especially Cindy Messina, for challenging me to bring forth the best within me. For their unconditional support and faith in my ability to accomplish this major endeavor, I acknowledge my friends, Gin and Warren Bedell, Jody and Hal Donnelly, Louise Weldon, Donna Kloppenburg, Cheryl Morand and Gaile Buice, as well as my brother and his wife, David and Daun Ledwell. A special thanks to Jody and Hal for facilitating the writing process by allowing me to use their home and computer on my writing adventures. I thank my business associates, Tricia Molloy, Sandy Bowers, Ann Cohan and Tom Schlinkert for their encouragement and interest in my work. I greatly appreciate the word processing assistance given to me by Sandra Bevilacqua. Thanks to Ann Mather for the expert advice she shared with me when I first began this project. I acknowledge Peter Vegso and Gary Seidler as well as the staff at Health Communications, Inc., for their willingness to take this risk. Thanks to Barbara Nichols for recognizing the value of this work early on. I appreciate Christine Belleris, her efforts, and her enthusiasm for this project she inherited. To Solveig Lamberg, the copy editor, who critically reviewed this work, I am grateful. I am humbled by the power of the Spirit Within, my Higher Self, because of whom seemingly impossible accomplishments have been realized. Thanks to each of you who helped make this vision a reality, for believing in me and for validating the gifts I am privileged to share.

Contents

PART ONE

THE BASICS

1
Living InSync
A Practical Philosophy

- *What are you willing to do to get more out of your life?*
- *Do you want to maximize your potential?*
- *Do you want to enjoy life more?*
- *Are you willing to move out of your "comfort zone?"*
- *Are you willing to be responsible for your feelings, thoughts, actions and decisions?*
- *Are you willing to take a risk, to be different from the crowd?*
- *Are you willing to put effort along with your desire to have more, be more and feel more?*
- *Are you willing to make mistakes?*
- *Are you willing to risk moving ahead with your life, letting go of the past and recycling that energy?*
- *Are you willing to be in gentle control of your life and your being?*
- *Are you willing to become proactive rather than reactive?*
- *Are you willing to tap into your personal power?*

If the majority of your responses to these questions is yes, then this book could be just the tool you've been looking for. Responding to the challenges presented here will open up unlimited opportunities for you to strive to become your best. Learning how to live InSync can be the key to experiencing and expressing your best self.

Living InSync is a concept and a philosophy. According to M. Scott Peck's definition, "one's view of the world," it's even a religion. Living InSync is more than abstract principles. It's a way of life, a way of living and a lifelong process. InSync as philosophy, religion and process exemplifies the mind-body-spirit interconnectedness in our lives. The essence of being InSync is found in the five dimensions of life.

Maintaining a balance among and within the dimensions of our lives offers us a perpetual challenge. Our being exists to evolve, our nature is dynamic and ever-changing. The static state of perfection desired by many is nonexistent. The continual flow of energy offers us infinite opportunities for learning about our selves and about others if we are willing to take the risk. By moving out of our "comfort zones," we can strive to be our best. We can have a vision of what we want to be. We can be in *gentle* control of our lives. We can combine the dynamic energies of desire, effort, determination, perseverance and patience to get what we want.

As you can see, living InSync isn't for the weak or the lazy! It isn't for those who expect everything in life to be fair. It isn't for those who want to receive without giving. It isn't for those who expect their needs and wants to be met by others. It isn't for those who want and expect perfection. Only those who want the best that life has to offer will take the risk to be their best. Only those who are willing to take on the challenge of living InSync will maximize their potential. Striving to be our best is the most worthy of all pursuits. Are you ready to accept this challenge? Then read on.

LIVING INSYNC

InSync is accessing and optimizing your personal power, understanding your self and others, envisioning what you want in life and pursuing goals that will help you be the person you want to be. When you access your personal power, you use your mental capacity for making creative decisions, being productive and being in *gentle* control of your life. Your emotional, mental, physical, social and spiritual dimensions continually evolve in harmony. When these are in balance, they create the harmonious music of your life.

Understanding Myself

InSync is understanding who you are so you can have a better understanding of others. Truly seeking the truth about oneself is kind of tough, isn't it? When we closely and critically scrutinize our selves by examining our human beingness, we feel quite uncomfortable. Examining your self requires moving out of your comfort zone. It's much more comfortable to maintain the social and public self and to believe that the person others want us to be is the person we are.

Being the person that others want and expect us to be takes some of the responsibility of being our true selves off our shoulders. We don't have to think too much about making decisions. We don't have to make any major changes. We don't have to rock any boats or ruffle any feathers by doing something differently or not doing anything at all. We just follow the script we've been handed and life moves merrily along with little joy and false contentment. We accept our lot in life. There's no reason to move out of one's comfort zone because knowing what to expect is most comforting.

But wait! Is living out another's expectations really living? If you really want to live, you must take the risk and move out of your comfort zone in search of the real you. Growth requires movement and change.

Understanding Others

We are social beings—we need other people. I can only understand you and what makes you unique to the extent that I understand my self. The more I understand my self, the more I can understand and empathize with you. The more I recognize that your best adds to, and does not detract from, my best, the more I can celebrate both of our personal accomplishments and victories. This understanding contributes to creating the harmony you want in life. When you understand others, you recognize their perspectives, their challenges, their uniqueness, their worth, their value to this universe and your own life. Without this recognition, there is no understanding, and there is no living InSync.

Envisioning What You Want in Life

What does your future look like? Can you imagine what you'll be like? Do you have a plan for where you'll be and for those tangible and intangible things and qualities you'll possess? Can you look beyond where you are right now and see where you can be if you really want to be there? InSync is envisioning your future clearly. When your vision is not crystal clear, your life may feel ambiguous, muddled, foggy and directionless. Often you might see your self in the fulfillment of someone else's vision. If you want to develop and nurture your vision, being in *gentle* control of your life is essential. Being in *gentle* control requires focus. Focus comes from being intimately in tune with your self. It comes from eliminating extraneous variables in your life. Focus comes from listening to your gut, your intuition, the still small voice within your self.

If you can vividly imagine your self in the future, the likelihood of your future looking the way you've designed it is possible. If you can't see your self in a particular situation or place in the future, it won't happen. When you vividly imagine what you want, your subconscious mind enables you to focus your desires by sensitizing you to beneficial opportunities that come your way. Into your awareness comes new perspectives and insights that will take you closer to your goal of being your best. To go after what you want in your life and to be in the places where you want to be is being in the process of living InSync.

Pursuing Goals

In order to get what you want in life, you must put action with your desires and your vision. Action comes through setting and pursuing goals. Goals come in all shapes and sizes. Goals often represent milestones in your life—completing school, finding a job, getting married, buying a home. Goals also come in the form of New Year's resolutions that are made and broken on the same day and in the form of dreams that "Someday I'll . . ." It's not enough to have wishes, desires, dreams, or even goals.

Unless you structure your desires and pursue them with passion, the desires are never realized. You have to apply effort, determination and patience to your dreams. You must stick with your pursuit no matter what. You must *wait* for your good to come to you. In short, getting what we want requires work. The pursuit always pays off.

The value often comes from unexpected sources. Life-changing experiences and opportunities can only present themselves while we're in the process of pursuing our best. There's no formula. There's no easy route. How you perceive the pursuit can bring you understanding, growth and joy or your perceptions can bring you despair. This message is about growth and maximizing the joy of the journey.

You may be saying to your self, "Well, I've set goals in the past and I never got what I wanted." There are many reasons we don't reach goals we set. Some of those reasons have to do with the circumstances and not with the effort we've put forth. Sometimes the goals are too big. We become overwhelmed and give up rather than breaking down the goal into smaller goals that can reasonably be achieved. Goals are not reached because we don't make them priorities. We don't allocate sufficient time, energy and resources to make them work. Sometimes the goals we select are not truly our goals, but goals others have told us would be good for us. We lack emotional commitment to those. Without commitment, no goal can be realized.

The critical process in goal setting is working through obstacles that stand in the way of getting where you want to go. Goals change over time because you change. Think about goals that you had when you were younger. Do they match with where you are now? In many cases, the goals you have for your self now are different from the goals that you had three years ago. Your current goals more than likely differ significantly from the goals you had when you were 18.

Not all goals are realized. Even those you can clearly visualize in your mind's eye may not come to fruition. Achieving our goals often depends on others to behave in a certain way or to respond in a favorable manner. Circumstances necessary for us to reach our goals are not always there, preventing us from getting where we wanted to go in the way we planned. Frequently, we don't have adequate resources or support for reaching goals. There are times when the goal no longer holds the allure it did when we first set it. We change and so do our goals.

At times it's appropriate to abandon a goal we've set for our selves. The goal may no longer be good for us. Abandoning certain goals often leads to freedom. When you release a goal that's no longer working for you, your energy is freed to move faster and more fully in the direction that you need to go. Living one day at a time is important. Investing in your life one day at a time is vital.

Using Your Mental Capacity

When you're InSync, you exercise your mental capacity. Everything you do, feel, perceive and think is managed by the brain. Using the brain, you can do whatever it is that you want. Your highly intricate and complex brain is as individualistic as you are.

According to the latest research, we use less than 1 percent of our brain's capacity. Think of all that has been accomplished using such an incredibly small portion of our collective mental capacity. We've explored the depths of the ocean and the vastness of the universe. We've performed surgery with light, discovered cures for illnesses, interpreted unknown languages and eliminated perceptual barriers.

The brain empowers us and gives us the know-how and energy to get whatever we want out of life. By acknowledging and attending to the power of your mental capacity, you can maximize the use of your time, energy and resources. You can create opportunities, ideas and things that you've believed were out of your reach. You can explore the many options that are open to you when you make those tough decisions. Using your mental capacity empowers you to increase your productivity and to maintain *gentle* control of your life.

Making Creative Decisions

When we use our mental capacity without restraint, we're capable of making creative decisions. Unfortunately, we've developed inhibitions and created road blocks for our selves because somebody along the way has told us "You can't do that." Even when we'd argue for our own case and say, "Yes, I can," we'd hear a loud and strong note of discouragement saying, "No, you can't." Consequently we've developed endless audio loops in our heads that tell us repeatedly we can't do things. At a deeper level we know we can. As we know and experience life, there may be some limitations to what we can actually do. Yet, if we'd remove the barriers we and others have created, then our abilities to become more creative in our lives would be evident.

Each of us has the capacity for making creative decisions.

However, we often avoid making decisions of any kind because we're afraid we're going to be wrong. We don't like to be wrong. We don't like to venture out into the unknown. We're looking for a sure thing. We feel we've failed if our decision doesn't work out the way we expected it to.

Consider the case of Thomas Edison, the master inventor of the light bulb. On one bright and early morning, he didn't wake up and say to himself, "I think I'll invent the light bulb today, and it'll be perfect in every way." It took Edison an estimated 1,000 experiments to create the light bulb. His peers didn't understand his perseverance. I expect they asked questions such as, "Why do you keep doing this? You keep failing over and over and over again. When are you going to give up? Why do you keep beating a dead horse?" It is reported that Edison pointed out that his experiments were not failures, asserting that "I found 1,000 ways not to make a light bulb." It's important to keep in mind that each attempt at doing something new—which creates change in your life and in the lives of others—is not failure. You learn from each of your mistakes. You have the capacity to be creative when you choose to remove the barriers that block your creativity.

Increasing Productivity

As human beings we seem to have an innate drive to be increasingly productive in our day-to-day lives. We constantly complain about the lack we feel. We lack enough time to get things done. We lack the energy to do anything for our selves at the end of a busy work day. We lack the resources to do what we want and need to do. When we're living InSync, we can increase our productivity and eliminate the lack in our lives. We can indeed have a fuller life, both personally and professionally.

Wanting to be your best demands that you establish priorities. When you have priorities, their presence will drive your use of time, energy and resources. By focusing on your priorities, you'll find that you can eliminate unnecessary activities.

You can say "no" to others' requests for your time. You can delegate responsibility. You can settle for less-than-perfect performance in non-priority activities, and you can create resources to meet your desires and needs.

To increase your productivity, you need to become an effective and efficient time manager. Plan your days, and then work your plan. Set aside nondiscretionary time for unforeseen activities, such as traffic jams. Set aside time for your self to nurture your self, to stay in close communion with the person you are and the person you are becoming. Set aside time for play. By using your time wisely, you'll have the energy you need to get what you want completed. And by trusting your ability to access your mental capacity, you'll be creative in maximizing the resources available to you. You'll capitalize on those resources that you previously thought were unavailable.

Being in *Gentle* Control

Being in control of one's life is imperative. We generally associate control with structure, power, rigidity and being in charge. Some of us are excessively controlling our lives and the lives of others around us. We find our selves in uncomfortable places today because we don't want to give up any control. We feel we have to keep a tight reign on all of our actions, thoughts, feelings and decisions. Yet, when you're in the process of living InSync, you will find that being in *gentle* control of your life will further your efforts toward realizing your vision and attaining your goals. You'll plan your activities *and* allow for consideration of other opportunities that come your way.

Your life, like that of a symphony, is made up of many components. Some parts are similar and some distinctly different. Think of your self as the conductor of your life, in *gentle* control, consciously choosing to be flexible and adaptable. The symphony's conductor seeks harmony and creativity from the musicians. Isn't that what you really want? Gently controlling the many elements of life creates harmony and balance. This fundamental and continual integration of your multifaceted essence is the foundation of living InSync.

THE FIVE DIMENSIONS

We are multidimensional beings constantly seeking meaning and balance in life. The InSync philosophy embodies five dimensions: spiritual, physical, mental, social and emotional. These are the parts of our whole being. When we are living InSync, the dimensions work together so that we have harmony and balance in our lives. Here's a brief synopsis of each dimension. We'll more fully investigate each dimension in later chapters of this book.

The Spiritual Dimension

We are spiritual beings. The Spiritual Dimension empowers all of the dimensions and life itself. As the foundation for all of our desires, power and energy, our spirit nurtures the relationship we have with the source of our inner power. Many people define this source as "God," "Allah," or "Christ." The label you assign to your source is secondary in importance to the acknowledgment, respect and honor you give to this all-powerful entity.

You may be asking your self, "Is this a religious thing?" It's only a religious thing if you want it to be. You must decide what your spirituality means to you.

The Emotional Dimension

We are emotional beings. The Emotional Dimension represents feelings: acknowledging, accepting and appropriately expressing all of our emotions including joy, sorrow, delight and anger. When we think about emotions, many thoughts and feelings arise. Some of us enjoy our emotions, feeling happy and sad and sharing these feelings with others. Some of us would prefer not to have to consider emotions because they seem to get in the way. They come up at inopportune times for seemingly no apparent reason. Keep in mind that emotions are neither good nor bad, positive nor negative. Emotions just are. They are essential for our being. Every emotion is important. Every emotion communicates to us how the world is affecting us.

The Mental Dimension

We are mental beings. The Mental Dimension controls all the other dimensions because we have knowledge of our world as a result of thought. Thought results from the use of our mental capacity. Our brain controls our thoughts, feelings and behaviors. By responding to what we know about our selves and the universe, we define our direction and purpose in life. Setting and pursuing goals gives our visions definition and possibilities.

The Physical Dimension

We are physical beings. Taking care of our physical bodies is the major thrust of the Physical Dimension. We must give value to the role the body plays in our lives. It's the vehicle through which we're able to do whatever we choose to do. The body works in tandem with the other dimensions of our lives. Proper maintenance of our bodies is imperative.

The Social Dimension

We are social beings. Relationships are the foundation of the Social Dimension. The relationships we develop and nurture with our families, life partners, lovers, friends, co-workers and acquaintances represent an outgrowth of the individuals we are becoming. We can only develop healthy and nurturing relationships to the extent that we our selves are healthy and nurturing.

Our relationships are defined by how we nurture and

understand others, how openly we communicate, and how we give and accept support.

THE BASIC CONCEPTS

Being in *Gentle* Control

Are you conducting the music of your life's symphony? Are you directing the different aspects of your being? Do you take the rigid control approach, struggling to maintain control of everything and everybody in your life? Do you feel a tremendous sense of anxiety when your controlling behavior is counterproductive and yields the opposite result of what you really want? Or do you take a lackadaisical approach to your life, believing that whatever will be, will be? Do you believe that you're just a pawn in this great game of life and that you really have no say about what you really want or what you receive? Do you believe your fate is in the stars and that nothing you can do will make a difference so you don't do anything? Do you fluctuate between the two extremes, being in rigid control one moment and lacking any control the next? You do have another choice.

You can choose to be in *gentle* control of your life—to be goal-directed and purpose-oriented in your attitudes, feelings, thoughts and actions. *Gentle* control means that you make conscious choices about what you do with your time, energy and resources. It means you know where you want to go, and you are what you want to be. It means you're flexible and open to opportunities that present themselves. You're willing to consider new possibilities to see if engaging in them will bring you closer to your destination. It means that if you slip, you get back on track without self-retribution. It means that you control only those things that you truly can control, not the things that are outside your realm of influence and responsibility.

Maintaining Balance

Do you live a well-balanced life? Are you at peace with your career, your social life, your health, your self-esteem and your spirituality all at the same time? Often you'll find that life is going the way you want it to in one area, such as your career, but is less than desirable in other areas, such as your relationships. If things are not okay on the home front, your performance at your job will be adversely affected. The reverse is also true. We can only be our best when we have dynamic balance in our lives.

There are many aspects to our being—so when we take care of one of them, we're in essence taking care of the other areas, too. The interconnectedness is certain. You may tend to compartmentalize your life, preventing one area from infiltrating another. Life doesn't work that way. The compartments are arbitrary walls we construct in order to maintain rigid control. What happens in one part of our life affects every other. If your primary focus is taking care of your body and you neglect the other aspects of your life, you're out of balance with your self, your relationships and the world. What happened to us in the past has an effect on our present and future. We are truly a composite of all of life's experiences, thoughts and feelings. Maintaining balance enables us to expand our horizons and fully experience each moment of life.

Valuing, Respecting and Understanding

Do you know some people who seem to have no redeemable qualities? Are there people that you wouldn't give the time of day to? In today's society, as in all societies, there are people we put in such a category. Do you sometimes put your self in this category, believing you have no value, no worth? Whether or not it's apparent to you, each person, including your self, is valuable and deserves to be treated with respect. The extent to which you value and respect your self is the extent to which you can value and respect others. The intrinsic value in each human being is inherent. It's often not apparent because society doesn't always provide an environment conducive to such revelations. We often fail to respect others because their value system differs from our own. Keep in mind that valuing and respecting others doesn't mean agreeing with them. When you respect another, you're respecting their right to make conscious choices about their lives. Your respect is not agreement or approval. Remember—everyone must find their own way. The more you get to know, value and understand your self, the more you understand and value others.

Making Conscious Choices

Who decides for you? Who makes your choices? If you're going out to eat with friends, do you leave it up to them to decide on the restaurant? Do you defer to another's judgment because you think your opinion isn't valid? Do you select clothing that someone else likes, even if you're not really comfortable with it, because you want to please them or because it's trendy? Do you eat donuts and drink coffee in the breakroom because they're there? Do you take a job that you really don't want because your family insists it's the right thing to do? Do you struggle with a dysfunctional relationship or go to church on Sundays because you're supposed to? You often find your self in situations that are unhealthy for you because you've given up your freedom of choice and your right to make choices about what's best for you. Making conscious choices about what you want and need is a significant way to improve your life.

There are some activities that don't require a conscious choice every time you encounter them. Your morning routine or driving a car is performed without having to make conscious choices. Routine is an efficient and effective way to take care of the basics each day. You must be careful that routine is not a substitute for those choices you *need* to make.

Being noncommittal can also be a conscious choice. If you agree on any restaurant your friend chooses, then do so consciously. The habit of doing things "just because" or because you've always done them that way are targets for change.

Moving Out of Your Comfort Zone

When was the last time you did something that you had no previous experience with? What was the force that compelled you to move forward? What obstacles did you have to overcome? What benefits did you receive? As children, we're quite in tune with experiencing newness as we explore the world around us. We learn and grow as we experience the new and unfamiliar. As we grow into adulthood we become settled in our way of doing things. We might say, "I've done it this way for 40 years. I don't see any reason to change now." Or "I didn't learn to swim as a youngster. I'm too old to learn now. What good would it do me anyway?" Or "I'm a steak and potato kind of person. Tofu will never pass these lips!" Or "I've lived here all of my life. Why would I want to go anywhere else?"

We are reluctant to move into unknown situations because we're afraid we might look silly attempting a new skill or we might not know anybody or we might not like the results. It takes courage to move out of our comfort zone because we don't know what will happen. We're unaware of the possibilities that are open to us until we push through the barrier of comfortableness.

Every time we step out of our comfort zone, we expand our awareness and horizons. We change, and our perspective is modified. We see the world a little bit differently because every new experience affects us in countless ways, some of which we're aware of and others that are quite subtle. The only way to maximize the use of our time, energy and resources is to continue the process of growth. The only way to grow is to move out of our comfort zone.

Being Your Number One Priority

What's the most important thing to you? If you were to

write down your priorities, what would be at the top of your list? Would family, God, your kids, your partner, your church and your pets be at the top? How about you? Would you find your self on your list? In order to live life InSync—to be your best — you need to examine your priorities.

You may think that putting your self first is selfish and egotistical. Take another look. When you are your number one priority, you have the energy and resources to address the other priorities in your life. If you're constantly putting others first, you'll get worn down, frustrated and become empty. You'll have nothing to give to others in spite of your efforts.

When you make your self your number one priority, attention to your spirituality must take precedence. By attending to your Spiritual Dimension, you'll be better equipped to effectively take care of life's other dimensions. Be number one for your self. Encourage others to be their number one priority, too.

Celebrating Mistakes

When you make a mistake, what does that mean? What do you think? What do you say to your self? How do you feel? What do others say about you? What do you do about it?

In our society, we hold to the idea that we should never make mistakes. That somehow we're flawed as human beings because we didn't do or say something perfectly. We erroneously believe that mistakes chip away at our ideal self. Yet, without mistakes, we'd never learn or grow. Think about the first time a baby wants to walk or the first time you sat on the seat of a bicycle ready for your first ride or that first romantically-intended kiss. We didn't do these things perfectly. We made a second attempt, then a third and a fourth until we became comfortable and more proficient with our new skill. We became more daring, eager to try out a new way of doing what we were learning. Our mistakes gave us strength and encouragement to move forward—to make other attempts.

Mistakes are our teachers. Without mistakes we would not learn and grow. We wouldn't expand our skills and knowledge past a rudimentary understanding of life. Mistakes are very patient teachers: when we don't learn the lesson the first time, they continue to show us until we learn. Celebrating mistakes is celebrating new knowledge, new awarenesses and new skills.

Granting Permission

Do you know that it's okay for you to do whatever it takes for you to be your best? Do you know that you really don't have to ask anybody for permission to move forward in your life? As youngsters, we were taught that we must ask permission to do just about everything. And as adults, we continue to wait until we've been given permission to move forward.

If you feel like you need someone's permission to make the changes you want in your life, then give your self permission. You can rightfully do anything you want to do with your life. The only approval you need is your own. You must answer only to your self for whatever you choose to think and feel and how you act. Go ahead. Give your self permission to embark on this journey to get the most out of your life, to live InSync and to be your best *right now.*

Investing in Your Life

The most important investment of your time, energy and resources you can make is in your self. You are the most important person you know. When you invest in your self, you're simultaneously making an investment in others and in the world. Now is the time to create your own reality.

2
The InSync Scale

When you want to make changes in your life it's a good idea to assess where you are in relationship to where you want to go. *The InSync Scale* is designed to determine where you are now in each of the five dimensions. It will give you a clear idea of where you stand in the emotional, mental, physical, social and spiritual aspects of your being. By responding to each item, you create a sense of how InSync your life is. You'll also be able to determine which dimensions of your life could benefit from more of your attention. Keep in mind that this is an awareness tool for you to gain information and insight about your self.

Directions: Check the boxes for ONLY those statements that you believe are true for your self *most of the time.* Add the number of checks in each column and put that number in the space at the bottom of the page. Then read the explanations that follow.

21

		A	B	C	D	E
1.	I have a clear vision of where I want to go with my life.	❑				
2.	I deal effectively with conflict.					❑
3.	I feel comfortable expressing whatever emotions I am feeling.		❑			
4.	I eat legumes, whole grains, vegetables and fruits.				❑	
5.	I'm open to learning about others' points of view.			❑		
6.	I scan my body for tension and stress.				❑	
7.	I prioritize my time and activities.			❑		
8.	I'm willing to move out of my "comfort zone."		❑			
9.	I find it possible to forgive my self and others.	❑				
10.	I listen when others speak.					❑
11.	I say positive comments to my self.		❑			
12.	I can laugh at my self.					❑
13.	I avoid eating foods with additives and preservatives.				❑	
14.	I feel I am productive in my work life.		❑			
15.	I nurture a relationship with my Higher Self.	❑				

Totals for each column ___ ___ ___ ___ ___

A   B   C   D   E

		A	B	C	D	E
16.	I'm willing to change my perspective as I receive new information.			❑		
17.	I realize everyone has a different point of view.					❑
18.	I trust others.	❑				
19.	I believe I am of precious worth.		❑			
20.	I enjoy life.					❑
21.	I refrain from smoking.				❑	
22.	I enjoy facing challenges.			❑		
23.	I drink adequate amounts of water.				❑	
24.	I have fun with my friends and family.					❑
25.	I eat a sufficient amount of dietary fiber.				❑	
26.	I would rather be me than anyone else.		❑			
27.	I know my purpose in life.	❑				
28.	I willingly give to others.					❑
29.	I limit the added sugars and salt in my diet.				❑	
30.	I consciously cooperate.					❑
31.	I love my self no matter what I do, think or feel.		❑			

Totals for each column

$\overline{}$ $\overline{}$ $\overline{}$ $\overline{}$ $\overline{}$

    A   B   C   D   E

		A	B	C	D	E
32.	I abandon goals that no longer work for me.			❑		
33.	I have a sense of direction in life.	❑				
34.	I feel there are enough hours in the day to do everything I want to do.			❑		
35.	I love my self regardless of what others think.		❑			
36.	I use alcohol in moderation, if at all.				❑	
37.	I recognize that everyone has a different view of the world.			❑		
38.	I plan each day and follow my plan.			❑		
39.	I treat others with dignity and respect.					❑
40.	I commend my self when I do well.		❑			
41.	I accept that I'm not perfect.	❑				
42.	I encourage others to share with me.					❑
43.	I maintain my ideal weight.				❑	
44.	When I make a mistake, I learn the lesson in it for me.	❑				
45.	I give my self special treats.		❑			

Totals for each column

___ ___ ___ ___ ___

A   B   C   D   E

		A	B	C	D	E
46.	I believe I deserve to have what I want in life.		❏			
47.	I look for ways to grow and develop as a person.			❏		
48.	My muscles hold up when I'm involved in a repetitive motion (chopping wood, raking, sweeping).				❏	
49.	I laugh often.					❏
50.	I celebrate my mistakes.	❏				
51.	I limit the fats in my diet.				❏	
52.	I trust my own intuition.	❏				
53.	I am able to say "no" to requests for my attention and time.			❏		
54.	I feel I am productive in my personal life.		❏			
55.	I feel good about the person I am.		❏			
56.	I maximize the use of my time, energy and resources.			❏		
57.	I love others unconditionally.					❏
58.	I nurture my own spirituality.	❏				
59.	I value others' right to be whoever they want to be.					❏
60.	I am physically strong.				❏	
61.	I like solving problems.			❏		

Totals for each column   __ __ __ __ __

                                                         A   B   C   D   E

		A	B	C	D	E
62.	I believe there's a power higher than my self.	❑				
63.	I have a process for making decisions.			❑		
64.	I allow others to work out their problems their own way.					❑
65.	I eat breakfast daily.				❑	
66.	I feel free to let it be known what I want and need from others.		❑			
67.	I eat only when I'm hungry.				❑	
68.	I'm willing to extend my self in relationships.					❑
69.	I look for opportunities to learn new information.			❑		
70.	I keep my focus sharp.	❑				
71.	I am decisive.			❑		
72.	I enjoy physical touch from my loved ones.					❑
73.	I treat my self with dignity and respect.		❑			
74.	My heart and lungs function efficiently when I'm involved in physical activity.				❑	
75.	I feel at peace with my self.	❑				

Totals for each column

—　—　—　—　—

A　B　C　D　E

		A	B	C	D	E
76.	I feel I am in control of my life.		❏			
77.	I feel like I have a realistic understanding of others.					❏
78.	I communicate openly with others.					❏
79.	I refuse to compromise my values.	❏				
80.	I exercise aerobically on a regular basis.				❏	
81.	I feel creative.			❏		
82.	I have a broad support system.					❏
83.	I allow my self to feel whatever emotion I'm feeling.		❏			
84.	I am organized so I can easily retrieve information.			❏		
85.	I feel grateful for all that I possess.	❏				
86.	My body is flexible (I can touch the floor without bending my knees.)				❏	
87.	I resolve my internal conflicts.			❏		
88.	I have a vision of being my best.	❏				
89.	I enjoy spending time alone.		❏			
90.	I limit my caffeine and cholesterol intake.				❏	

Totals for each column

	A	B	C	D	E
	___	___	___	___	___
	A	B	C	D	E

		A	B	C	D	E
91.	I express my gratitude to others.	❏				
92.	I have satisfying personal relationships.					❏
93.	I feel like I have a realistic understanding of my self.		❏			
94.	I have written goals.			❏		
95.	I feel at peace with others.	❏				
96.	The relationship between my lean muscle mass and body fat is healthy.				❏	
97.	I take time to reflect about my life.		❏			
98.	I can think of more than one answer for most questions.			❏		
99.	I rest and relax my body regularly.				❏	
100.	It's easy for me to be "in the moment."	❏				

Totals for each column   __ __ __ __ __

| | A | B | C | D | E |

GRAND TOTALS   __ __ __ __ __
FOR ALL 7 PAGES   A B C D E

Column A statements are related to the **Spiritual** Dimension.
Column B statements are related to the **Emotional** Dimension.
Column C statements are related to the **Mental** Dimension.
Column D statements are related to the **Physical** Dimension.
Column E statements are related to the **Social** Dimension.

NOW TRANSFER YOUR SCORES TO THE PROFILE.

THE INSYNC PROFILE

Instructions: Using the total number of responses in each dimension, shade the boxes that correspond with that number. Then check the statement that corresponds with your score. Now consider how you feel about each dimension.

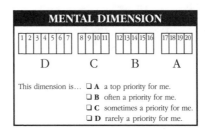

MENTAL DIMENSION

| 1 | 2 | 3 | 4 | 5 | 6 | 7 | | 8 | 9 | 10 | 11 | | 12 | 13 | 14 | 15 | 16 | | 17 | 18 | 19 | 20 |

D   C   B   A

This dimension is…   ❑ **A** a top priority for me.
❑ **B** often a priority for me.
❑ **C** sometimes a priority for me.
❑ **D** rarely a priority for me.

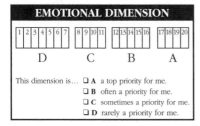

EMOTIONAL DIMENSION

| 1 | 2 | 3 | 4 | 5 | 6 | 7 | | 8 | 9 | 10 | 11 | | 12 | 13 | 14 | 15 | 16 | | 17 | 18 | 19 | 20 |

D   C   B   A

This dimension is…   ❑ **A** a top priority for me.
❑ **B** often a priority for me.
❑ **C** sometimes a priority for me.
❑ **D** rarely a priority for me.

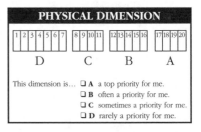

PHYSICAL DIMENSION

| 1 | 2 | 3 | 4 | 5 | 6 | 7 | | 8 | 9 | 10 | 11 | | 12 | 13 | 14 | 15 | 16 | | 17 | 18 | 19 | 20 |

D   C   B   A

This dimension is…   ❑ **A** a top priority for me.
❑ **B** often a priority for me.
❑ **C** sometimes a priority for me.
❑ **D** rarely a priority for me.

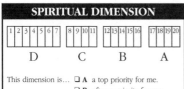

SPIRITUAL DIMENSION

| 1 | 2 | 3 | 4 | 5 | 6 | 7 | | 8 | 9 | 10 | 11 | | 12 | 13 | 14 | 15 | 16 | | 17 | 18 | 19 | 20 |

D   C   B   A

This dimension is…   ❑ **A** a top priority for me.
❑ **B** often a priority for me.
❑ **C** sometimes a priority for me.
❑ **D** rarely a priority for me.

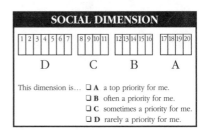

SOCIAL DIMENSION

| 1 | 2 | 3 | 4 | 5 | 6 | 7 | | 8 | 9 | 10 | 11 | | 12 | 13 | 14 | 15 | 16 | | 17 | 18 | 19 | 20 |

D   C   B   A

This dimension is…   ❑ **A** a top priority for me.
❑ **B** often a priority for me.
❑ **C** sometimes a priority for me.
❑ **D** rarely a priority for me.

Now that you know how InSync you are in each of the dimensions, you're ready to begin your venture of growing and living. The InSync Program is divided into each of the dimensions so you can go right to the exercises that will assist you in meeting your individual goals. If your "score" in the social dimension indicates that your relationships aren't InSync, you might want to start with those exercises now. Before you move into the program, you'll want to read Chapter 3, "Getting Started—Following Your Own Path."

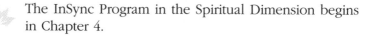 The InSync Program in the Spiritual Dimension begins in Chapter 4.

The InSync Program in the Emotional Dimension begins in Chapter 5.

The InSync Program in the Mental Dimension begins in Chapter 6.

The InSync Program in the Physical Dimension begins in Chapter 7.

The InSync Program in the Social Dimension begins in Chapter 8.

3
Getting Started– Following Your Own Path

Following your own path is not always as easy as it seems. It requires commitment and responsibility on your part. As you prepare for what you're about to experience, keep the following ideas in mind. These ideas will assist you through the exercises and will enable you to make your life what you really want it to be.

Recognize the Process

It takes more than desire and willingness on your part to live InSync. Keep in mind that living InSync, like life, is a

31

process. You never arrive at a point where you no longer have to put forth effort to be the kind of person you want to be or have the type of life you want. Ardent desire and incessant willingness must be coupled with your perpetual effort.

Be Gentle with Your Self

As you venture into living InSync, you'll find that some exercises will be more challenging than others. You'll also find that maintaining a certain practice may be difficult at first. Keep in mind that you're making changes in your life and that you're exploring new territory. Changes and exploration bring unknowns. Refrain from believing you'll know how to do everything perfectly the first time you try it. If an attempted change in habit doesn't turn out quite the way you want it to, encourage your self. Tell your self "I'm learning, I'll do it better next time." instead of "How stupid can I be? I knew I couldn't do that!" Maintain realistic expectations for your self.

Be Patient

When we know what we term as the "good life" is available to us, it's very difficult to wait for it to come to us. Sometimes we have to wait until circumstances can support what we desire. Our tendency is to want everything *right now*. We feel "I've done my part ... so where is it?" We want to give up. We don't see how things are working out on our behalf. As you're venturing into living InSync, remember that all of your efforts will yield the results you want ... in time.

Take One Step at a Time

When we learn about a new concept or idea, we get fired up, wanting everything to fall right into place. We want to change everything at once so we can enjoy the life we've envisioned. To avoid stress, disappointment and the feeling of being overwhelmed, do one exercise at a time. When you're comfortable with your progress, move on to the next one. Refrain from tackling too many changes all at once. It took many years to develop the habits you have now; changing them overnight is an unrealistic expectation. You'll find that some exercises, such as reducing your fat and cholesterol intake at the same time, go hand-in-hand. Taking one step at a time will get you where you want to go.

Celebrate Lessons Learned

With every new experience, mistakes will occur. Keep in mind those mistakes are your teachers. If you pay attention and learn the lesson when you make the mistake, you won't need to make it again. For example, in your enthusiasm to make your life more of what you want it to be, you may decide to make a daily plan and follow it. Then you may feel chained to your schedule because you feel compelled to follow it perfectly. You may find that you have no time for your self or that you didn't allocate enough time to a project or enough time for interruptions. The lessons from this might be to schedule time for your self, to schedule flex-time, and to allocate 30 percent more time to a project than you think it will take. (Things always take longer than we think they're going to.) Then celebrate what you learn.

Expect Discomfort

Moving out of your comfort zone will bring you discomfort. It's inevitable. Discomfort occurs because you'll have a tendency to desire the time when life was somewhat easier and certainly more predictable. The discomfort will arise from changes in your own thoughts and feelings, as well as those that are shared with you by others. For example, let's say you're currently a "junk food junkie" and you've decided you want to eat healthier foods. Expect resistance. Resistance will cause you discomfort. When you opt for fresh fruit rather than coffee and donuts for your morning snack, you may experience ribbing from your partner or co-workers. You'll find that, at least at first, it's really more convenient to eat whatever's around rather than being responsible for bringing your own snack.

It takes time to change the habit you've had for years. The voice inside your head will remind you of the other changes you've wanted to make in your life that didn't work out. Be strong. When you experience the discomfort, remind your self that you're making an investment in your self and that the changes will take you closer to your goal. Get comfortable with the uncomfortableness.

Expect Greatness

Me? Greatness? Yes! You'll experience greatness because greatness comes in all sizes and forms and most often when you least expect it. Greatness is achieved when you move beyond your old self and into a new level of awareness and understanding. Greatness comes from simple acts of kindness, knowing and understanding. We're not always aware of our moments of greatness—they often occur without our knowing. Yet, from time to time, another person will tell us how we've impacted their lives, how we've made their journey a little easier, how we shared with them in an unselfish manner. When we hear these words, we are reminded of our greatness.

Greatness also comes to us in subtle realizations about our selves. Think of the "ah-has" you've experienced in life. By exercising in the various dimensions, you'll experience many "ah-has." Greatness is often as subtle as it is grand. Greatness is yours, so expect it.

Know You're in Control

Once you take the responsibility to invest in your own life, you're in control. Being in control doesn't mean that everything will go as you plan it or as you want it to be. You have total control only over *your* actions, thoughts, attitudes and how you deal with your feelings. In many cases you cannot exercise any control over circumstances or other people. Keep in mind that you do control what your response is to others and to circumstances. In the midst of seeming confusion and uncertainty, you can control the way you think, act and respond to your feelings. And how you think, feel and act has a tremendous impact on others. That impact often changes circumstances and other people's points of view.

You Can Be Your Best

Being your best is stretching and reaching beyond mediocrity, beyond the routine. It's refusing to accept the status quo as the only answer to life's questions. Being your best means you're open to opportunities for growth and development, and that you're consistently striving for the next level of understanding and intuitive knowing. It is knowing that when you're at your best others can also choose to be at their best. While you're venturing in The InSync Program you may hear a little voice inside your head saying that your goal of being your best is an impossible dream. Don't listen to it! Your rebuttal most assuredly is: "I can be my best." Know that your best changes as you experience new learning and growth opportunities. You are your *best* right now. Tomorrow you can be a different *best* if you consciously make that choice.

Expect Setbacks

With progress comes setbacks. Setbacks occur because you're adjusting to your new way of thinking and your new way of doing things. When the challenge becomes more than you feel you have the strength to handle, you lapse into old patterns of behavior. Often the magnitude of your setback reflects the importance of the changes you're making. When the setbacks occur, recognize them for what they are, reminding your self that human beings have setbacks when they're making changes in their lives. Reaffirm your commitment to your self, and move forward. Remember, the setback often keeps you apprised of how much progress you're making.

Enjoy the Process

The process of life is full of mysteries to be uncovered and adventures to be experienced. And what could be more adventuresome than getting what you want out of your life? As you make this important commitment to your self, there will be times when you'll feel discouraged and even overwhelmed. Look for the fun in the process. Look for the small lessons you've learned and the unusual manner in which some situations work themselves out. Laugh at the absurdities you witness. Laugh when you find your self in a difficult position. Growth and learning require much effort. Enjoy your new experiences and discoveries.

Commend Your Self

All of us like to receive recognition for doing a commendable job. You'll want to find ways to commend your self for following through with your commitment. What can you do to recognize your efforts as you move from one exercise to the next? What can you give your self that will remind you of your worthiness and the value of the investment you're making in your life? It's different for everyone. Find what works for you. Naturally, you'll want to vary the ways you commend your self. The intangible can be more satisfying than the tangible. (*Avoid using food to commend your self.*) Just be sure you consciously choose to give your self the recognition you deserve.

Stick to It

When we initially decide to delve into a new project we're enthusiastic and eager to move ahead. We don't let minor discouragements get in our way. Then we're faced with obstacles that overwhelm and demand our attention. When the struggle requires a lot of energy we often decide to just give up. Don't let those obstacles hinder you from getting what you deserve to have in life. Stick to your plan! If you're frustrated in one dimension of your life, pursue opportunities in another until you've generated the energy to go forward. Sometimes you need a break because you lose your perspective. Your new way of thinking needs time to incubate before new ideas are accepted. Whatever you do, once you've decided to follow your own path, persevere! You're charting new territory. The breakthrough is just ahead if you keep your commitment. Remember—persistence pays off.

Recognize Its Worth

As you move along the uncharted course, keep in mind the value of what you're doing. Remember that you're making the most important investment of your time, energy and resources that you could possibly make. You're investing in your self, and that means you'll have so much more to give others. By being your best you'll help others be their best. Whatever you do to get what you want out of life is beneficial to others just as it is beneficial for you.

Possibilities Are Limitless

What you can accomplish with your life is limitless. Your wildest dreams can be realized if you're willing to make the commitment and put forth the effort that is necessary to impact your reality. What will you choose to do with your life? What do you want more than anything else? Begin *right now* to make conscious choices about what you want and exercise *gentle* control in your life.

The InSync Program is waiting for you!

PART TWO

THE INSYNC PROGRAM

DIRECTIONS FOR PARTICIPATING IN THE
INSYNC PROGRAM

Following these directions will assist you in maximizing the benefits you'll receive by experiencing the InSync Program exercises. Each exercise is set up in the same format: a synopsis; a reflection about past experiences and the feelings associated with those experiences; suggested exercises for a new experience and fresh perspective; an acknowledgment of a new awareness and understanding; and a resolution to follow through with a plan for action. There's space for you to write down your thoughts if you'd like. Here's the recommended process to follow:

1. Read the introductory synopsis.
2. Think about your own previous experiences with the topic.
3. Think about how you felt about those experiences.
4. Read the suggested exercise(s).
5. Think about what doing this exercise means to you.
6. Consider your options and develop your plan for action.
7. Put your plan in writing and into action.

Now's the time to make conscious choices about your life. Get ready to move out of your "comfort zone" and enjoy learning more about your true self.

4
Growing InSync with the Spiritual Dimension

Whatever you believe about how you came to be, there is an energy, a force, a Power that's greater than you that created the conditions for you to be here on earth. How you define this energy is personal and ultimately the most significant part of your being. When you acknowledge and nurture that energy, you realize this Power also defines you. The very essence of your being is altered and enriched when your spiritual dimension receives attention and care.

Where do we find spirituality? It's in nature, in the kind acts of others, and most importantly within our selves. In the quietness, we commune with the Power that gives us purpose and energy to be our best, to give our best, and to maximize our potential.

Your spiritual dimension is the foundation for the other dimensions of your life. You must first acknowledge that you are a spiritual being. Whatever you choose to believe about your spiritual nature dramatically and significantly affects how you live, how you feel your emotions, how you use your mental capacity, how you take care of your body, and how you interact with others. Without a firm foundation in the spiritual dimension, maintaining balance and wholeness within your self is impossible.

Key exercises in this section introduce you to the spiritual dimension of your life. These include acknowledging your Higher Power and nurturing your spirituality. Envisioning your best, knowing and living with purpose in life and accepting your humanness are also explored. You can also learn to forgive and trust your self and others. Being at peace, celebrating the child within as well as your mistakes, following your intuition, staying focused and expressing your gratitude are also examined.

ACKNOWLEDGING MY HIGHER POWER

Your Higher Power creates and sustains the essence of your being. That source of energy gives you purpose, motivation to move forward with confidence and the vision for being your best.

No matter what religious orientation you have or where you believe your Higher Power "lives," your relationship with your Higher Power is an intimately personal one that you must define for your self. No religious or philosophical doctrine or dogma can dictate how your relationship must unfold. This Power is your inner source of direction, strength, courage and wisdom. Refrain from getting "hung up" on the label others give to this Higher Power. Choose whatever label is meaningful for you.

Your ability to deal effectively with the challenges in your life is greatly enhanced by your awareness and belief that you're not alone, that you live life with a silent partner who leads and guides you along your path. No doubt you can go through life as well as death without coming to grips with your Power or even acknowledging its existence; but your spark, zeal and enthusiasm for life, for being and doing your best, for understanding your self and others and for sharing your gifts, will be flat. Only when we recognize we're not sufficient unto our selves and that there's a greater power or energy source that's responsible for our presence here on earth, can we truly know our selves, maximize our potential and have a positive life-giving influence on others.

My Previous Experiences With Acknowledging My Higher Power

Reflect on what you have just read and your own experiences with acknowledging your Higher Power. You might want to jot down some thoughts as they occur to you.

My Feelings About These Experiences

Think about the feelings you have as you acknowledge your Higher Power. Write them down.

Suggested Exercise

Take some quiet time to examine your thoughts and feelings about your Higher Power. What do you really believe about your Higher Power's existence in your life? How do you refer to this Higher Power? What kind of relationship do you have now? Are you allowing that relationship to work fully for your benefit? Are you able to understand the impact this has on every moment of your existence? From time to time, revisit these questions and contemplate your responses.

Exploring My Understanding

Complete the following sentence: To me, *acknowledging my Higher Power* means . . .

Considering My Options

Complete the following sentence: NOW I'm going to . . .

NURTURING MY SPIRITUALITY

For anything to grow and develop, we must nurture it. The same is true for spirituality. If we want to be in better touch with our essence, we need to expend time, energy and resources to discover the core of our being.

Think of your spiritual nature as a garden that requires the tilling of soil, the planting of seeds, the feeding and watering of plants, weeding and harvesting. You must be involved in a continuous process to maintain a healthy and growing garden that reaps great benefits at harvest time. So it is with your spiritual-ity. The soil is the essence of your being. The seeds are the dreams, aspirations and purpose. You feed and water your spir-itual garden with thoughts, ideas and emotions that nourish the connection with your Higher Power. The weeding is getting rid of negativity and old baggage. It's letting go of past hurts and pains. It's removing worry about things that will never come to pass. When you reap the fruits of your spiritual harvest, you are sharing your gifts, talents and abilities with others.

You're bringing to fruition what your spiritual nature is all about — being in full communion with your self so that you can be in full communion with others. By nurturing your spir-ituality, you're bringing to life the vision of being your best and fulfilling your purpose in life so you can indeed become what you choose to be and do what you choose to do with your life. You have direction and purpose.

My Previous Experiences With Nurturing My Spirituality

Reflect on the experiences of nurturing your spirituality. Make notes as your thoughts occur to you.

My Feelings About These Experiences

Think about the feelings you have as you nurture your spir-ituality. Write them down.

Suggested Exercises

1. Take a few moments every day to sit in the quiet and just be with your self and your Higher Power. Listen for that inner voice that affirms and gives you guidance.

2. Begin an Affirmation Collection. Create a notecard file of affirming statements that are meaningful, uplifting and inspiring for you. These statements can come from material that you read, your goal statements, or other ideas that you generate as a result of your awareness and insight. Read each card at least once a day, in the morning during your quiet time, while waiting in line, while commuting (but not driving), in the evenings or whatever time of day that works best for you. By attending to the thoughts on your cards, you're affirming your spiritual nature. You can also create an audio tape of your affirmation which you can listen to while driving. You may add and delete affirmations as time goes on.

Exploring My Understanding

Complete the following sentence: To me, *nurturing my spirituality* means . . .

Considering My Options

Complete the following sentence: NOW I'm going to . . .

KNOWING & LIVING WITH PURPOSE

Every thought, feeling and action has its origin in purpose. The purpose may be as rudimentary as seeing what it's like to entertain a particular thought. As human beings we search for meaning in life because *purpose* is inherent to our nature. We always want to make sense out of a feeling, a situation or even a revelation. When our transitory purposes are connected to one central purpose, our behavior becomes more meaningful and more goal-directed, leading to the attainment of our desires.

The source for knowing your purpose in life is found in the intimate relationship you experience with your Higher Power. There's a reason for your existence here on earth at this particular point in time. Your fundamental purpose is to make a positive impact on the lives of others. Your gifts and talents are used to fulfill that purpose.

The knowing is revealed in the quiet. Purpose reveals itself when you are open and ready to accept it. Your purpose guides the use of your abilities, gifts and talents, which may include discovering a cure for a disease, spending time with a person who finds herself in circumstances that are less fortunate than yours, sharing a message of hope and love through song, or treating all people with dignity and respect.

When you're aware of your purpose for being, it's easier to make choices about what to do with your time, energy, and resources. With purpose foremost in your mind, you can relate all of your decisions to it. We are moved to action when our direction is clear and aspirations are passionate. This drive adds meaning and energy to our thoughts, feelings, and actions. Being cognizant of purpose, direction, and aspirations lends a sense of wholeness to one's view of the world. By keeping your focus on your purpose—what you're all about—you can get what you want out of life and share your gifts with others.

My Previous Experiences With Knowing & Living With Purpose

Think about your experiences with knowing your purpose in life. Write down your thoughts as they occur to you.

My Feelings About These Experiences

Think about the feelings you have as you experience knowing and living with purpose. Write them down.

Suggested Exercises

1. In the quiet, ask your Higher Power to reveal what your purpose is by indicating your willingness and readiness to receive the answer. Once you've asked, be confident that the response you requested will be revealed to you. It may come immediately while you're sitting in the quiet. It may come later while you're leisurely walking on the beach or when you're exercising or driving your car. Your purpose may be revealed to you when you're working on a project or communicating with a friend. The key to knowing your purpose is to maintain a spirit of readiness along with a willingness to recognize your talents. Knowing requires patience.
2. To remind your self to live with purpose daily, write this question on cards or pieces of paper and post them in conspicuous places: *"Are my thoughts, feelings, and behaviors on purpose today?"*

Exploring My Understanding

Complete the following sentence: To me, *knowing and living with purpose* means . . .

Considering My Options

Complete the following sentence: NOW I'm going to . . .

ENVISIONING MY BEST

When you consider what your "best" looks like, what do you see? Is your vision one that others have created and imposed upon you *(you're so talented in..., you should...)* or is it one that is a natural outgrowth of the relationship you enjoy with your Higher Power? Having a clear vision about what you want to do with your life and how you want it to be is a key element in getting what you want. Keeping that vision clear and in the forefront of your mind facilitates your ability to make conscious choices. Your vision is the focal point for ideas, plans and actions. By maintaining an acute awareness of what the "end product" looks like, you can make choices about life with confidence. Keep in mind that your growth and development as a human being will continually modify your vision as you strive to be your best.

Being your best is a *process* and there is no final "end product." We can always make improvements, increase our awareness and embark on new journeys that will lead us to a higher understanding of our selves and others. Your best can be defined as seeing your self and others as unique human beings, maintaining an openness about life and striving to positively impact the lives of others. Do so in the absence of inhibitions and barriers that create a void between you and your Higher Power and between you and others in your life.

My Previous Experiences With Envisioning My Best

Think about the vision of your self that you have created. Write down your thoughts.

My Feelings About These Experiences

What do you feel as you envision your best? Write down your thoughts.

Suggested Exercise

You can do this exercise in your mind's eye using visualization. Fill your vision with colors, sounds, tastes, touches and smells *or* create a tangible representation of your vision. The purpose of the exercise is to elicit a response to the question, "What do I look like when I'm being my best?"

After you've created your representation of being your best, respond to the question, "How do I feel about being my best?" Keep this vision of your best crystal clear, resolute and dynamic. You'll stay focused and on target for being your best. Engage in this exercise from time to time, particularly when you make substantial changes in your life. Remember, the vision will likely change with time and as you learn from your experiences.

Exploring My Understanding

Complete the following sentence: To me, *envisioning my best* means . . .

Considering My Options

Complete the following sentence: NOW I'm going to . . .

AUTHENTICATING MY VALUES

Each of us holds a set of beliefs that are fundamental and at the root of all actions, thoughts and opinions about the world in which we live. Each of us makes decisions based on our fundamental beliefs and values. Values are inculcated from the very beginning of life. We learn our values from our parents and caretakers from what they say as well as what they do. All of our actions are predicated on what we believe. If we say one thing and do another, then what we truly value will be observed through our behavior. With values, actions speak louder than words. We typically inherit the same set of values our parents hold with little deviation, and we call them our own unless we make a conscious choice to change them.

My Previous Experiences With Authenticating My Values

Think about authenticating your values. Write down your thoughts.

My Feelings About These Experiences

What are your feelings about authenticating your values? Write them down.

Suggested Exercise

Make a list of the values held by your parents. Pay attention to what they said was important, and look closely at their actions. Now review the list. Put a circle around those values that you also hold to be true. Then ask your self what values you would choose if you were starting to build your value system from the beginning. If you identify some values that create dissonance for you, take action to make the changes you want to make. Make your values truly your own.

Exploring My Understanding

Complete the following sentence: To me, *authenticating my values* means . . .

Considering My Options

Complete the following sentence: NOW I'm going to . . .

ACCEPTING MY HUMANNESS

Although it's tough for most of us to accept, we are human beings first. By virtue of being human, we're also imperfect. Our imperfection manifests itself in what might be considered flaws in the beauty of our bodies, poor judgment, fallacies in our thought processes, under-utilization of the brain's capacity, etc. We often use great effort, particularly when it comes to our physical bodies, to change, so that part of our lives will be perfect. One of the fallacies regarding perfection is that there's a universal standard by which we can compare what is real and what is perfect. In reality, perfection can be whatever you want it to be.

We're reminded of our imperfection when we make mistakes, when we attempt a new skill for the first time and use it inappropriately. It's the denial of our humanness that creates the expectation that we should do everything perfectly on the first attempt. Our humanness shows up in the inconsistencies in our thoughts, behaviors, logic and commitments. We may not pursue the goal with the same fervor on a moment by moment basis. We make decisions based on incomplete information because it is not possible for us to know everything. Our humanness and imperfection are recognizable because our judgment is affected by our emotions and personal desires. We can rarely be totally objective.

Because of our humanness, we have purpose in life; we are the instruments through which the Higher Power works. Accepting our humanness relieves feelings of frustration that result from attempting to be everything and do everything perfectly. We come to realize that our contribution to life is both great and small in the big scheme of reality. We are compelled to come to terms with our mortality, knowing that each breath we breathe is a gift, and that there are no assurances of the future. When we accept our humanness, we strengthen the spiritual connection. Reminded of the source of our strength, we're energized to impact people's lives in the here and now.

My Previous Experiences With Accepting My Humanness

Think about how you accept your humanness. Write down your thoughts.

My Feelings About These Experiences

What are your feelings about your acceptance of your humanness. Write down your feelings.

Suggested Exercise

When you don't meet your own expectations of being and doing your best, rather than beating your self up, acknowledge your humanness with "That's the human in me!"

Exploring My Understanding

Complete the following sentence: To me, *accepting my humanness* means . . .

Considering My Options

Complete the following sentence: NOW I'm going to . . .

CELEBRATING MY CHILD WITHIN

"You're becoming an adult now. You must put away childish things" was the message we heard. The absence of our child is noted when we lose our appetite for curiosity, become unwilling to take a risk, lose confidence in our selves, and let fear stand in their way of being who we want to be and getting what we want. Regardless of what you heard and believe, your child is alive—curious and eager to enjoy life as well as explore and learn! When we believe in our selves, we celebrate our child within. Believing in your self gives you the impetus to experience the new, to risk others' disapproval, to risk failure as well as success. With confidence you can build your desire to grow and experience life to its fullest. You can expand your realm of knowledge and your view of the world. Your heightened awareness will give you a better understanding of your self as well as others. When you believe in your self, you willingly and enthusiastically celebrate the child within you. You take the risk to explore those childhood issues that you've previously ignored. You're willing to come to grips with the past so you can enjoy each present moment and move forward into the future. By exploring your world, enjoying life, attending to your needs and fulfilling your desires, you celebrate your child within.

My Previous Experiences With Celebrating My Child Within

Think about your experiences with celebrating the child within. Write down your experiences.

My Feelings About These Experiences

What do you feel about these experiences? Write down your feelings.

Suggested Exercises

1. Spend some time playing with a young child between the ages of two and six. Let him or her lead the play time. When play time is over, think about what you experienced and what you learned.

2. When you're feeling stagnant, uncreative and bored, do something that's child-oriented. Here are some suggestions to get your started: build a sand castle, ride a merry-go-round, swing, read a children's story, see a Disney movie, buy something for your self at a toy store, eat a snow cone, get your face painted.

3. If you have issues that are unresolved from your child-

hood, seek assistance from qualified professionals. Seek out one you feel very comfortable with so you can explore your issues, release them and move forward in life.

Exploring My Understanding

Complete the following sentence: To me, *celebrating my child within* means . . .

Considering My Options

Complete the following sentence: NOW I'm going to . . .

FORGIVING MY SELF

Unforgiveness comes from a desire for and expectation of perfection. When you're unforgiving of your self, your creativity is inhibited, your willingness to take risks is squelched, and your willingness to move out of your comfort zone is restricted. Your unforgivingness interferes with your relationships with your Higher Power, your self and others. You tend to engage in self-defeating behaviors, such as not taking care of your body or restricting your self from enjoyable experiences because you feel you don't deserve anything better. In essence, you deny respect for your self.

When you choose to forgive your self, you're not denying

what happened. Neither are you absolving your self of the responsibility for your thoughts, emotions, actions and their consequences. When you choose to forgive your self, you are accepting your humanness and giving up the struggle over your imperfections. You release pent up energy that can be used in moving forward with your life. Whatever you have done in the past cannot be undone. What you can do is learn the lesson and move on. You have every right to forgive your self. You deserve another opportunity to "clean the slate" and begin again.

My Previous Experiences With Forgiving My Self

Do you forgive yourself? Think about how you experience this. Write down your thoughts.

My Feelings About These Experiences

How do you feel about this experience? Write down your feelings.

Suggested Exercise

On a piece of paper, first write down something for which you've not forgiven your self. Then determine what the benefit has been for holding on to that unforgiveness. Write that down. Next, think about what you will gain by forgiving your self and write that down. Finally, determine what you will lose when you forgive your self and write that down also. With this information, make a conscious choice to decide what action will benefit you the most. Then take the action you choose. Keep in mind that when you forgive your self, the energy you've expended to hang on to the unforgiveness will be freed and useful in moving you closer to what you want out of life.

Exploring My Understanding

Complete the following sentence: To me, *forgiving my self* means . . .

Considering My Options

Complete the following sentence: NOW I'm going to . . .

FORGIVING OTHERS

We hang on to the unforgiveness we have for others because we don't want to forget how we were violated. We believe that keeping the "wrong" alive will serve as protection. It'll make us cautious and keep us on the lookout for other perpetrators.

Nurturing an unforgiveness fortifies the wall we've erected between our selves and others. We send the message, "I won't ever be treated like that again." When we continue to create a void between us and others because of our unwillingness to forgive, our lives are negatively affected. Our willingness to develop intimate relationships is restricted and our energy and enthusiasm for life is depleted.

Forgiveness is an act we do to benefit our selves, not something we do for others. When we forgive others, we are not denying what occurred. We're putting the event in perspective. We're releasing the hold it has had on us. We're releasing the emotional sting and withdrawing our emotional attachment to it. We're acknowledging the other person's humanness and their natural inclination to make mistakes. When we forgive others we're affirming that we're moving on with our lives—a stronger human being for overcoming the hurt and rising above the experience.

My Previous Experiences With Forgiving Others

Think about forgiving others. Write down your thoughts.

My Feelings About These Experiences

What do you feel about forgiving others? Write down your feelings.

Suggested Exercise

On a piece of paper, identify one person against whom you hold an unforgiveness and how they violated your rights. Then determine what the benefit has been for you to hold on to that unforgiveness and write it down. Next, think about what you

you will gain by forgiving that person. Write that down. Finally, determine what you will lose when you forgive him or her. Write that down also. With this information, make a conscious choice about what action is the most beneficial for you. If your decision is to forgive, then mentally, emotionally and/or symbolically release that unforgiveness. (It is not recommended that you tell the person you've forgiven them. If you're still in contact with them, they will know by your actions.) By releasing the unforgiveness, you're freeing pent up energy which can now be used to nurture new and developing relationships. You can use this process for any unforgiveness you are holding onto.

Exploring My Understanding

Complete the following sentence: To me, *forgiving others* means . . .

Considering My Options

Complete the following: NOW I'm going to . . .

TRUSTING MY SELF

We have a tendency to lack trust in our ability to "get the job done." We believe that other people can do things faster, better and more effectively than we can. We believe that what we have to offer isn't good enough to meet others' expectations. We lack confidence in our ability to use the talents and gifts that we've been given by our Higher Power. When we lack trust in our selves, we're denying our spiritual connection and attempting to deal with life's challenges on our own.

The benefits of trusting your self are large in magnitude and wide in scope. When you trust your self, you honor your inner power by recognizing it as the source of your strength. You are acclaiming that the use of your abilities can make a difference in people's lives. You acknowledge your ability to use good judgment when you make decisions. You recognize your uniqueness. You affirm your right to learn from the mistakes you make. When you trust your self, you're willing to fully listen to the internal as well as eternal wisdom of your intuitive self. By trusting your self, you demonstrate your faith in the omnipotence of your Higher Power.

My Previous Experiences With Trusting My Self

Write down your experiences with trusting your self.

My Feelings About These Experiences

Write down your feelings about these experiences.

Suggested Exercise

The next time you learn that someone is seeking a person with a skill you have for a particular project (it could be work, community, family, etc.), ask your self if this is a project you'd like to be involved in. If your answer is "yes," volunteer your efforts. Rather than telling your self that someone else could probably do this better, tell your self how fortunate this team is to have you on board for this project. Remind your self that no one can make the kind of contribution you're making. Also celebrate the opportunity you have to use your skills.

Exploring My Understanding

Complete the following sentence: To me, *trusting my self* means . . .

Considering My Options

Complete the following sentence: NOW I'm going to . . .

TRUSTING OTHERS

Lacking trust in others' abilities to deliver is a result of the experiences we had with people who betrayed us, failed to meet our expectations, sent us mixed messages and took advantage of our time, energy and resources. Often we find that our energies are stifled because of these experiences. We keep the experiences alive in our minds to remember to use extreme caution when interacting with others. When we trust others we risk disappointment, rejection and hurt.

If we superimpose our feelings and knowledge about a prior situation on a person we're interacting with, our behavior stems from prior experience rather than responding to the current situation. If we predetermine that this person will interact with and treat us as he has before, we don't give him a chance to be himself, and we can not relate to him with a fresh perspective.

To get what you want in life, you'll benefit greatly from learning how to trust others. Other people make significant contributions, so you can get what you want. This is not to suggest that you indiscriminately trust other people with your time, energy and resources. Rather, it's a suggestion to learn about people on a person-by-person, situation-by-situation basis so you can make a conscious choice about your willingness to trust. Always listen to your inner knowing—to your intuition. That wisdom will assist you in making the best choice for you.

My Previous Experiences With Trusting Others

Write down your thoughts about trusting others.

My Feelings About These Experiences

Write down your feelings about trusting others.

Suggested Exercise

Remove the words "always" and "never" from your daily vocabulary. If you hold to the belief that someone *always* does everything the same way, such as ignoring you, letting you down, falling down on the job, etc., then you have difficulty maintaining a clear, objective perspective when you interact with this person the next time. The same line of thinking holds true for *never*. If you believe "they never . . . ," then you're unwilling to give them the benefit of any doubt. Monitor how removing these words from your vocabulary affects your view of and interactions with those people who up to this point "always-did" and "never-did" according to your experience.

Exploring My Understanding

Complete the following sentence: To me, *trusting others* means . . .

Considering My Options

Complete the following sentence: NOW I'm going to . . .

FOLLOWING MY INTUITION

How many times have you made a decision with your head and failed to listen to your inner knowledge, your gut, your intuition? You feel it when you start to do something that isn't right for you. We often feel our intuition gnawing away when we're making decisions or choices about our lives. Yet we often ignore what we're feeling because we think our minds know best. After all, we weighed the advantages, disadvantages and the consequences. The choice we made seemed to make sense to us.

When we ignore our intuition, we frequently make choices that are not best for us. We deny input from our Higher Power, we don't trust our selves, we don't see how things could possibly work out because we can't see beyond appearances. We go with what we know, ignoring that we can't possibly know everything about any situation.

Our intuition serves as a subtle silent alarm. When it "rings" it expects us to listen and then prompts us to respond accordingly. You must be willing to contrast what you "know" to be the right thing to do and what your intuition is leading you to do. Following your intuition requires taking a risk and putting aside a heavy reliance on what appear to be the facts. When you follow your intuition, the result of your action will prove to be most beneficial for you.

My Previous Experiences With Following My Intuition

Write about your experiences with following your intuition.

My Feelings About These Experiences

Write about your feelings of following your intuition.

Suggested Exercises

1. When you are in the process of making a decision, do the mental work, look at the options, the advantages and disadvantages and the possible consequences.

After you've made your preliminary decision, find a comfortable position and ask your self if the decision you're making is the right one for you. Listen for the response. If the response doesn't come immediately, let your intuition know that you are willing to receive the answer. Then stay attuned with your self so you'll "hear" the response when it comes. In addition to the quiet time you spend with your intuition, other conducive conditions may include being in nature and exercising your body.

2. To remind your self of the important role that intuition plays in your life, take a few moments to think about situations in which you ignored your intuition, your gut feeling, about something. What was the outcome of your decision? For what reasons did you choose to ignore your intuition? How did that decision impact your life? After you've thought about a few of these situations, make a commitment to yourself to listen to your intuition when you make choices about what you want.

Exploring My Understanding

Complete the following sentence: To me, *following my intuition* means . . .

Considering My Options

Complete the following sentence: NOW I'm going to . . .

PRACTICING PATIENCE

Patience—waiting for your expectations to be met—is a most difficult ability to master. We live in an instant gratification society where information, meals, products and services are rendered within minutes of our requests and 24-hour stores are becoming more and more abundant. We expect our needs to be met, our desires to be fulfilled and our expectations to be realized on the spot.

Waiting for what we want is difficult when we're not willing to go through the process. Time allows the process to fully unfold. You may say to your self, "Well, if I can't have instant happiness right now, then I just don't want to fool with it," or "If I can't maintain a balanced lifestyle without a whole lot of effort, then I'm not that interested."

We forget that getting what we need and expect takes time and often depends on the actions of others. We are perhaps too frequently reminded that people operate using their own timing. What seems urgent to you may be a low priority for someone else. Think of patience as being an investment in your success. Remind your self that all things and all relationships that are of value take time to grow and develop from the thought seeds you plant. Patience is accepting your purpose in life and knowing you will have whatever it is you need to fulfill your purpose, to meet your needs, to satisfy your desires and to get what you want out of life. Patience is trusting your intuition to make the best choices for you.

My Previous Experiences With Practicing Patience

Write down your experiences with practicing patience.

My Feelings About These Experiences

Write down your feelings about practicing patience.

Suggested Exercise

Plant some seeds in soil. Fertilize and water them. On a calendar, make daily notes about the changes you observe. Once the seeds have matured into plants, review the daily notes you've been keeping. Reflect on the relationship this plant has to your own life.

Exploring My Understanding

Complete the following sentence: To me, *practicing patience* means . . .

Considering My Options

Complete the following sentence: NOW I'm going to . . .

CELEBRATING MISTAKES

Mistakes are invaluable teachers of the lessons of life. Without them, we'd know very little about what life has to offer. Our experiences would be rather limited. We'd never experience taking risks or moving out of our comfort zones. Making mistakes is something most of us don't really like to do, yet they serve at least two purposes: First, they remind us of our humanness—that we really aren't perfect, and second, they are vehicles to learning important lessons in life. Think about a time when you celebrated knowing something new about your self or learned a new skill that resulted from doing something incorrectly the first, second, or third time around. It's okay to be imperfect.

My Previous Experiences With Celebrating Mistakes

Think about celebrating your mistakes. Write down your thoughts.

My Feelings About These Experiences

What do you feel about celebrating your mistakes? Write down your feelings.

Suggested Exercise

Here is a process you can use to learn how to benefit from your mistakes. When you make a mistake:

1. Admit you made the mistake.
2. Look for the lesson that is embedded in the mistake. "What's the lesson in this mistake for me?"

3. Make a plan so you won't make the same mistake again. "How can I avoid making the same mistake again?"
4. Feel pleased that you learned something new. "I celebrate knowing..." (Fill in the blank with what you have learned about your self.)

Exploring My Understanding

Complete the following sentence: To me, *celebrating my mistakes* means . . .

Considering My Options

Complete the following sentence: NOW I'm going to . . .

STAYING FOCUSED

In hectic day-to-day activities, it is often difficult to stay focused on what you're all about. There are many distractions that pull on your time, energy and resources. You often feel stretched between doing what you want to do, doing what you have to do and doing what others want you to do. At times you give in to the pressures others place on you because you feel you don't have the strength or the right to say "no" to their requests or deserve the time you want for your self.

If you really want to achieve what you desire in life, it's critical that you find ways to stay focused. In order to stay focused, you must have clearly defined goals and priorities. Having them in place will give you an anchor that will help you maintain a stable foundation for your life.

To stay focused you must know who you are. You learn about who you are from spending quiet time with your self, by listening to your intuition, by taking time to communicate with your innermost being and by nurturing the relationship you have with your Higher Power. When things are hectic, you always have a place you can come back to—a place to know and feel this is the real you, "This is what I'm all about."

My Previous Experiences With Staying Focused

Write down your thoughts about staying focused.

My Feelings About These Experiences

Write down your feelings about staying focused.

Suggested Exercises

1. Spend "quiet time" with your self. Get into a comfortable position and release the concerns you feel about what's happening around you. Think about what you're all about. Reflect on your priorities and your goals. Think about your relationship with your self and with your Higher Power. After you affirm the path you're on, then just be with your self as you breathe life-giving breaths. Let all thoughts float away. Feel the calm and

peace that comes with taking just a few moments for your self. It's recommended that you take some "quiet time" first thing in the morning, last thing in the evening and then anytime during the day when you're feeling stretched and overwhelmed. The amount of time you spend doing this exercise is entirely up to you.

2. Write your goals and priorities on cards that you can post and keep handy. Use color when making your cards. When you're feeling out of control of your situation, look at your cards. Then make a conscious choice about what you need to do.

Exploring My Understanding

Complete the following sentence: To me, *staying focused* means . . .

Considering My Options

Complete the following sentence: NOW I'm going to . . .

EXPRESSING MY GRATITUDE

We have much to be grateful for: life, good health, a sound mind, people who care about us, healing and the necessities of life. Yet, we often neglect to let our selves and others know how much we truly appreciate the time, energy and resources they've invested in us. Frequently, we can't see the things we

need to be grateful for because we feel we don't deserve someone else's generosity. We believe we have to earn the good
things in life, or we have to prove we are worthy of another's
gift. At times we don't feel "good enough" to enjoy life's gifts.

As creations of our Higher Power, we are worthy human
beings and indeed deserve all the good things we receive and
more.

We can express our gratitude in a number of ways. We say
"thanks," give a hug, send cards and notes or give a tangible
gift. We can also express our appreciation for life and what we
possess by sharing our talents and gifts with others. Are you a
pianist who plays music for the kids in the neighborhood on
Saturday afternoons? Do you grow flowers and then give them
to people who have assisted you in some way?

We all have gifts that are not fully expressed. One way to
fully express your gifts is to share them. You receive more
when you recognize your worthiness to receive gifts of all sizes,
both tangible and intangible. You also receive more when you
recognize your responsibility for sharing with others. In giving
of your self and your gifts, you receive abundantly.

My Previous Experiences With Expressing My Gratitude

Write about your experiences with expressing gratitude.

My Feelings About These Experiences

Write about your feelings when you express gratitude.

Suggested Exercises

1. For a full 24 hours each week, consciously express gratitude to everyone—including yourself and your Higher Power—who does something for you no matter how minuscule. You'll feel blessed and richer for the experience.

2. Think about how you share your gifts with others. Keep in mind that in giving you also receive. Look for ways to share your gifts in a way that is healthy for you as well as beneficial for others.

3. Give your self a gift just for being you and for no particular reason. Savor the feelings you have for being recognized for just being your self.

Exploring My Understanding

Complete the following sentence: To me, *expressing my gratitude* means . . .

Considering My Options

Complete the following sentence: NOW I'm going to . . .

BEING AT PEACE WITH MY SELF

We're not guaranteed any additional time in life with the exception of what we're experiencing at this very moment. When we put off what we want and need to do, we shortchange our selves and the experiences we can have.

Being at peace with your self is a state of being one's best. It means that conflicts are resolved and you're satisfied that you're being and doing the best you can at that particular moment in life.

When you're at peace, you refrain from worrying about those things you have no control over, you allow others to be responsible for their own lives and you're content that you've treated your self and others with dignity and respect. You're confident that you're sharing your talents and gifts with those who need and appreciate them and that you accept your self as the unique human being that you are. You're comfortable with where you are in life, with your accomplishments, with your efforts and, most importantly, with who you are *right now*. Being at peace means you've released grudges and unforgiveness toward your self and others. It means you are firmly centered in being your self.

My Previous Experiences With Being At Peace With My Self

Write down your thoughts about being at peace with your self.

My Feelings About These Experiences

Write down your feelings about being at peace with your self.

Suggested Exercise

Set aside quiet time in the morning to prepare for the day. In a special place, get into a comfortable and relaxing position. Close your eyes and clear your mind of the thoughts that surround the day's activities. Make affirming statements to your self. Then spend a few silent moments just being still and quiet. Take deep breaths. With each breath, feel a sense of peace and calm as you prepare for the day.

In the evening, think about those things that went well during the day. Examine the lessons that were learned from the mistakes that were made. Then spend a few quiet moments breathing deeply and just being. Keep in mind that being at peace with your self is not about doing; it's about being comfortable with your inner being and the way that comfortableness manifests in your life.

Exploring My Understanding

Complete the following sentence: To me, *being at peace with my self* means . . .

Considering My Options

Complete the following sentence: NOW I'm going to . . .

READER/CUSTOMER CARE SURVEY

If you are enjoying this book, please help us serve you better and meet your changing needs by taking a few minutes to complete this survey. Please fold it & drop it in the mail. **As a thank you, we will send you a gift.**

Name: _____

Address: _____

_____

Tel. # _____

Gender: ____ Female ____ Male

Age: ____ 18-25   ____ 46-55
____ 26-35   ____ 56-65
____ 36-45   ____ 65+

Marital Status: ____ Married ____ Single
____ Divorced ____ Partner

Is this book: ____ Purchased for self?
____ Purchased for others?
____ Received as gift?

How did you find out about this book?

____ Catalog
____ Store Display
Newspaper
____ Best Seller List
____ Article/Book Review
____ Advertisement
Magazine
____ Feature Article
____ Book Review
____ Advertisement
____ Word of Mouth
____ T.V./Talk Show (Specify) _____
____ Radio/Talk Show (Specify) _____
____ Professional Referral _____
____ Other (Specify) _____

What subject areas do you enjoy reading most? (Rank in order of enjoyment)

____ Women's Issues   ____ New Age
____ Business Self Help   ____ Aging
____ Relationships   ____ Altern. Healing
____ Inspiration   ____ Parenting
____ Soul/Spirituality   ____ Diet/Nutrition
____ Recovery   ____ Exercise/Health
____ Other (Specify) _____

What do you look for when choosing a personal growth book? (Rank in order of importance)

____ Subject   ____ Author
____ Title   ____ Price
____ Cover Design   ____ In Store Location
____ Other (Specify) _____

When do you buy books? (Rank in order of importance)

____ Xmas   ____ Father's Day
____ Valentines Day   ____ Summer Reading
____ Birthday   ____ Thanksgiving
____ Mother's Day
____ Other (Specify) _____

Where do you buy your books? (Rank in order of frequency of purchases)

____ Bookstore   ____ Book Club
____ Price Club   ____ Mail Order
____ Department Store   ____ T.V. Shopping
____ Supermarket   ____ Airport
____ Health Food Store   ____ Drug Store
____ Gift Store   ____ Other (Specify)

Additional comments you would like to make to help us serve you better.

_____
_____
_____

Thank You !!

5

Growing InSync with the Emotional Dimension

Emotions are an essential part of your being. Every emotion is important. Every emotion conveys the impact life experiences have on you. When you think about emotions, many thoughts and feelings arise. You may enjoy being an emotional being, laughing and crying with others, responding to others with your heart. Or you may prefer to ignore your emotions because they seem to get in the way. They come up at inopportune times for no apparent reason. You may be willing to do anything to avoid them. The tendency is to enjoy experiencing the "good" emotions and despair when you're experiencing the "bad" ones. In reality, emotions are emotions, neither good nor bad.

Your emotions are interconnected with the other dimensions of your life. There is a physiological response to how you feel. Joy, happiness, delight, contentment and love have a positive physiological effect; you seek to prolong these feelings as long as possible. Anger, hate, disgust, jealousy and disappointment cause a stressful physiological reaction. These feelings don't make us feel "good." There's an urge to act on the feelings—to get rid of them—to satisfy the need to purge the mind and body of the "bad" feelings. The body is negatively impacted when the emotions are not experienced and dealt with in a timely fashion.

Refusing to experience your emotions affects you spiritually, mentally and socially as well. When you fully experience your emotions, you are truly celebrating your humanness. You're in touch with the core of your essence because you're free from the inhibitions that result from ignoring your emotional dimension. Mentally, you experience sharper and clearer thinking. You're able to see a situation with more objectivity and make decisions with more confidence.

Your relationships are enhanced because of the freedom you feel in expressing your self to those who are important to you. You're more willing to develop richer and closer relationships, to experience intimacy and to put your self in a position with another where it feels safe to be vulnerable.

Emotions wield power over the more logical and rational side of our nature. At times we prefer the rational and logical side because we can predict outcomes and find reasons for why things exist as they do. We make decisions based on fact, not on feelings. Yet, without the balance of our emotional and mental dimensions, we are out of sync with our true nature. Both dimensions must be fully developed in order to live a fulfilled life.

Although it's usually not socially acceptable to acknowledge, accept and appropriately express emotions (especially for men), attention to this dimension in our lives is critical. Emotions give you the energy to move forward in daily life and the drive to stretch beyond everyday accomplishments. Emotions, such as passion and enthusiasm, are the critical elements in the enjoyment of life. Exercises to be explored in the emotional dimension include valuing your self, treating your self with dignity and respect, feeling and expressing emotions. Identifying inherent needs and freedoms, indulging your self and setting aside time for reflection will also be addressed. We will also explore talking to your self positively, celebrating your uniqueness and loving your self unconditionally.

Please refer to page 40 for directions on how to maximize your experiences.

VALUING MY SELF

Each of us is unique, unrepeatable and of precious worth. So how come we don't feel that way? How we value our selves is a direct result of how we perceive others value us. It's a direct result of the experiences we've had from the time of our birth.

Many of us attach our value to how smart we are, how much money we make, how many degrees we can put behind our names, how successful we are in our chosen careers and other attributes and skills that have no true impact on how worthy and valuable we are. Our inherent value comes from the reality that we are human beings. Our mere humanness gives us value that is priceless. Our true value is intrinsic and unrelated to what we can do.

We often feel we have nothing different to contribute to society, that there's nothing special about us, that we have nothing that anyone else has an interest in. These feelings come from misperceptions about what is true and what is of value. No matter what we think or what others may tell us, we have many gifts and talents that we can share with others. We feel, think and respond to the world around us by the way we value our selves. The more we share, the more valuable our gifts become and the more extensively the benefits from using our gifts and talents will be felt.

My Previous Experiences With Valuing My Self

Write down your experience with valuing your self.

My Feelings About These Experiences

Write down your feelings about these experiences.

Suggested Exercise

Set aside some time to think about your uniqueness, worth, strengths, attributes and skills. Consider these questions:

- How am I different from others?
- What contribution do I make to society?
- How have my actions benefited others?
- What have I done that has enriched another's life?
- What is it that I can contribute better than anyone else I know?

After taking some time for contemplation, draw a picture, make a collage, make a list or form a clay figure or whatever form is comfortable for you, to symbolize your value to your self and others. Display your project in a convenient place so you can add to it as you think of other ways in which you have value. Every time you look at your project, think of your own value and repeat to your self with enthusiasm and confidence, "I am unique, unrepeatable and of precious worth."

Exploring My Understanding

Complete the following sentence: To me, *valuing my self* means . . .

Considering My Options

Complete the following sentence: NOW I'm going to . . .

TREATING MY SELF WITH DIGNITY AND RESPECT

When you feel and show respect for another, it's often the result of your experience with that person. You regard them as having worth, feel you can trust them, have confidence in them and most often agree with them on basic fundamental issues.

The tell-tale sign of whether or not you have respect for others is found in your behavior during your interactions with them. Your behavior and attitude are the true determinant factors in how you feel about another.

What about respect for your self? How do you regard your self? How do you behave toward you? How do you allow others to treat you? Do you exercise, nourish, rest and relax your body? Do you nurture your spiritual nature? Do you fully experience your emotions? Or do you rob your body of needed rest and proper nutrition? Do you call on your spiritual nature only in times of distress? Do you stifle your emotions? Do you deny your own needs in deference to those of others? Do you "beat your self up" with criticizing and devaluing remarks when you've made a mistake or done something that didn't receive the approval (from your self or others) you expected? Do you allow others to violate your rights because you don't feel worthy enough to stand up for your self?

Respect for yourself is vitally important. Without high regard for your own "beingness," you'll refrain from nurturing your self and meeting your own needs. If you deny your self the respect you deserve, you devalue your worth to your self and to society.

My Previous Experiences With Respecting My Self

Write about your experiences with respecting your self.

My Feelings About These Experiences

Write about your feelings with these experiences.

Suggested Exercise

To take a closer look at the extent to which you respect your self, make a list of ways you show respect and the ways you show disrespect for your self. Think about the circumstances and your behavior.

- How do you know when you're being respectful?
- How do you know when you're being disrespectful?
- How do you feel when you're respectful toward your self?

- How do you feel when you show disrespect toward your self?

Examine the reasons for your disrespectful treatment. Then select at least two ways you can treat your self with more respect. Make a plan to do so. Then several times a day, particularly when you're not feeling very respectful about your self, affirm, "I treat my self with dignity and respect."

Exploring My Understanding

Complete the following sentence: To me, *treating my self with dignity and respect* means . . .

Considering My Options

Complete the following sentence: NOW I'm going to . . .

LOVING MY SELF UNCONDITIONALLY

Loving your self is tough because it's likely you can reel off more than a few things about your self that you don't like very much. And loving your self unconditionally feels impossible at times. It's imperative if you want to love others unconditionally.

Loving your self unconditionally means that you accept your self for who you are no matter what. It's not based on whether you've been good or perfect or met your own or someone else's expectations. Loving your self unconditionally means that you have value even when you err.

Loving your self unconditionally allows you to transcend the belief that you must do "good works" or be the "perfect" friend or spouse. You deserve love because you're alive! You deserve its healing ingredient in all of your relationships, including the one with your self.

My Previous Experiences With Loving My Self Unconditionally

Write down your experiences with loving your self unconditionally.

My Feelings About These Experiences

Write down your feelings about these experiences.

Suggested Exercise

Write your self a love letter and sign it affectionately. Tell your self how you feel about being you. Share with your self what makes you special. Elaborate on your gifts. Reveal your innermost thoughts. Put the letter in a self-addressed stamped envelope and mail it. You'll be delighted when you receive it and read the loving words you wrote to your self. You may want to consider repeating this process from time to time. It's a great way to remind your self of your importance and your love for your self.

Exploring My Understanding

Complete the following sentence: To me, *loving my self unconditionally* means . . .

Considering My Options

Complete the following sentence: NOW I'm going to . . .

FEELING MY EMOTIONS

Emotions are a part of us that we don't always understand. We don't always enjoy feeling every emotion that is generated by our present and past experiences. Emotions tend to get in the way when we've rationally analyzed our options making an important decision.

Many of us were denied experiencing the emotions we felt. Historically, boys weren't supposed to feel sadness or pain. Girls weren't supposed to feel anger or disappointment. Often we were told we shouldn't feel a certain way. Consequently, as adults, many of us have difficulty feeling anger and sadness as well as knowing it's our right to experience any way we feel.

Our minds remind us that experiencing these feelings is contrary to what we've always been told. We tend to avoid feeling the "bad" feelings because we've learned that something must be wrong with us if we feel badly about a certain situation. We want to extend the "good" feelings and do whatever is pleasurable and euphoric. We neglect to recognize and accept that we're a composite of emotions that brings us joy as well as sadness, sorrow and pain.

It is when we fully experience our emotions that we are fully human. Sometimes we find that the slightest thought or incident brings about feelings we're unfamiliar with or ones we can't understand. Sometimes, there is no rational reason for our feelings. It's important to experience whatever we feel about any given situation. Giving our selves permission to do so is important. By experiencing our emotions, they are released, making way for other feelings and opening the way for clarity in our thinking. It's important for us to experience whatever it is we feel and to fully appreciate this aspect of our being.

My Previous Experiences With Feeling My Emotions

Write down your experiences with feeling your emotions.

My Feelings About These Experiences

Write down your feelings about these experiences.

Suggested Exercise

Spend some time with your emotions. Perhaps you'll want to set aside a day to focus on experiencing whatever you're feeling. The following activities can serve as a catalyst for bringing emotions into your awareness. Keep in mind that any experience brings emotions with it. So add your own activities to this list.

1. Watch a movie or television program, such as the reruns of "Little House on the Prairie" or "MASH."
2. Walk in nature.
3. Listen to a mother reprimand her child in the grocery store.
4. Get a call from a friend canceling a date.
5. Witness a marriage ceremony.
6. Read a children's book.
7. Watch a documentary about hunger, AIDS or violations of civil rights.
8. Watch a couple embrace.
9. Attend a very competitive sporting event.
10. Watch a Little League softball game.
11. Smell fresh bread just removed from the oven.

While you're involved in the activity, fully experience whatever emotions you're feeling. The label isn't that important. After your "feeling" experience, release the emotions. Then take a few minutes to reflect on your experience. Here are some suggested questions you can ask your self:

- How did fully experiencing your emotions feel?
- What conflicting feelings did you have?
- Why do some emotions feel uncomfortable whereas others feel terrific?
- How did fully experiencing the event or activity provide you with more information about your self?

You may want to use this exercise from time to time to develop a habit of feeling your emotions.

Exploring My Understanding

Complete the following sentence: To me, *feeling my emotions* means . . .

Considering My Options

Complete the following sentence: NOW I'm going to . . .

EXPRESSING MY EMOTIONS

Many of us feel great emotion, but are hesitant to express how we feel. We're concerned that our feelings will be denied by others, thus invalidating our right to experience whatever it is we feel. We're not used to having permission to say what we feel. We're fearful our feelings will cause those we work with and those we care about to reject us. We believe we have to defer to others' opinions and feelings. We recall times when we've expressed our emotions, perhaps inappropriately, and were humiliated for doing so. Therefore, we often choose not to express our emotions to lessen the risk of rejection, humiliation, embarrassment and fear.

Expressing emotions, whether they be happiness, disappointment, love, anger or fear, is critical to the full evolution of who you are. Your expression helps you to relieve tension and reduce stress. If you remind your self that it's okay to experience whatever it is you feel, you'll be more secure and appropriate in expressing your emotions. By expressing how you feel, you reveal an integral aspect of your being to your self and to others.

My Previous Experiences With Expressing My Emotions

Write down your experiences with expressing your emotions.

My Feelings About These Experiences

Write down your feelings about these experiences.

Suggested Exercises

1. Keep a log of how you feel about your self, others and situations you find your self in. Write in the log anytime you want to express your self or work out how you feel in a particular situation.

2. Stimulate your artistic abilities. Express your feelings through art, dance, needlework, music, poetry, etc. Keep in mind you're expressing your emotions for your benefit, so other people's opinions about the quality or value of your expression isn't important. There's no reason for you to share your expression unless YOU WANT TO DO SO. If you decide to share, do so with those who support you and will offer encouragement as you learn more about your self.

3. Begin telling others in an appropriate way how you really feel. When someone asks you how you're feeling this morning, give them a response that truly reflects your feelings. If you feel uncomfortable with a discussion or decision that's being made, express your self: "I feel uncomfortable with . . ." (This exercise will take some practice. We're not used to expressing what we truly feel nor are people used to hearing how someone else truly feels!) Keep in mind that ease comes from practice.

Exploring My Understanding

Complete the following sentence: To me, *expressing my emotions* means . . .

Considering My Options

Complete the following sentence: NOW I'm going to . . .

ELIMINATING MY FEARS

Fear is powerful. We literally become prisoners of our fears. Fear inhibits us from experiencing new situations, getting involved in relationships, making decisions, dreaming, deciding what we want to do with our lives, eating a dessert, missing a workout or expressing our feelings and concerns. You can add your own fears to the list.

We're afraid of rejection. *Others won't accept me.* We're afraid of failure. *What if I do it wrong?* We're afraid of the unknown. *I've never done anything like that before.* We're afraid of criticism. *What if they think this is a stupid thing to do?* We're even afraid of success. *What will I do if I really make it?* There may be a logical reason for being fearful, such as being afraid of riding a motorcycle because you were involved in a serious accident. However, most fears are unpleasant figments of our imaginations. The results of research studies indicate that only about three percent of what we fear is within our control. Fear is most often **F**alse **E**xpectations **A**ppearing **R**eal. In reality, we use fear as an excuse for not getting what we need and want in our lives.

The power you've relinquished to your fears is a power that belongs to you. By eliminating your fears, you regain that power and control in your life. When you reclaim your power, you accept the responsibility for eliminating the obstacles that interfere with your success.

My Previous Experiences With Eliminating My Fears

Write down your experiences with eliminating your fears.

My Feelings About These Experiences

Write down your feelings about these experiences.

Suggested Exercises

1. Identify one of your fears. Write your fear down on the center of a piece of paper. Around this, write down your answers to the questions listed below. Realize that your answers may not surface immediately. You may need some time to process the questions and formulate the answers. Take whatever time you need, and refrain from demanding immediate answers from your self. Once you've taken the time to closely examine your fear, you'll be ready to eliminate it from your life.

    a. What previous experience have I had with this situation?
    b. What is the reason for this fear?
    c. Why do I hold onto this fear?
    d. Why does this fear hold so much power over me?
    e. Am I using this fear as an excuse for not being responsible for my self?
    f. What will I gain from eliminating this fear from my life?

2. Take the direct approach. If you're fearful of water, take swimming, boating, skiing or scuba lessons. If you fear rejection when you meet new people, go to a social function at least once a week with a friend who can introduce you to others. Think of some interesting topics you can discuss. One of the best ways to engage others in conversation is to ask them about themselves. Questions that generally stimulate conversation include:
    - How long have you lived in this area?
    - What kind of work do you do?
    - What's your favorite vacation spot?
    - What's the most unusual experience you've ever had?

    You can add your own questions. The key to taking the direct approach in eliminating your fears is to learn what you need to know and practice in an environment that feels safe to you.

3. Use visualization. Close your eyes and clear your mind. Visualize your self in the fearful situation. Imagine your self doing whatever you have difficulty doing in reality. Make your picture very vivid: fill it up with colors, sounds, feelings, tastes, smells and textures. As you see your self engaging in the activity, feel confident and powerful. Use this visualization process as often as possible to help you build confidence and eliminate fear. Prior to engaging in the feared activity, take a couple of minutes to visualize your self doing it. Then use your gained confidence in the real situation.

Exploring My Understanding

Complete the following sentence: To me, *eliminating my fears* means . . .

Considering My Options

Complete the following sentence: NOW I'm going to . . .

DEALING WITH DISAPPOINTMENT

Experiencing disappointment is a fact of life. It's part of our humanness to feel disappointed when our expectations are not met and the realization of our desires is squelched. No matter how well we plan or how deeply we desire something, sometimes things just don't work out the way we want them to.

Since the success of most ventures depends on specific actions from others, we often forget they may not share the necessary level of emotional commitment. We can't undo what's happened. We can learn from the experience and make a conscious choice about how we're going to deal with the situation. You can choose to let disappointing outcomes defeat you or you can divert your energy into a new project or a new challenge.

My Previous Experiences With Dealing With Disappointment

Write down your experiences with dealing with disappointment.

My Feelings About These Experiences

Write down your feelings about these experiences.

Suggested Exercise

When you're dealing with a disappointing situation, use this process to help you move on:

1. Acknowledge the reality of the situation. Even when you don't agree with an outcome, keep in mind you can't undo what's been done. Recognizing what has happened, rather than denying it, is a key step in moving on.

2. Let your self experience what you feel. Although you may hear, "You shouldn't feel that way," it's always important to experience your feelings. Most disappointing situations bring with them a mixture of emotions, some that may be difficult to sort out. Even though your feelings don't make sense, it's critical that you have the opportunity to express them.

3. Evaluate the situation and look at it as objectively as possible, examining the role you played. Ask your self:
    *   What could I have done differently?
    *   Would it have been to my advantage to wait rather than push the issue?
    *   Were my expectations realistic?
    *   Was the success of this venture too dependent on others?

    Reflection and introspection will reveal much useful information about your self!

4. Learn whatever lesson you can. When things don't work out the way we want them to, there's usually something we need to learn about our selves or about how we communicate with others.

5. Move on. Rather than wallowing in self-pity, take the knowledge you've acquired from the situation and the lessons you've learned, and use them to move ahead. Make conscious choices about the direction you want to take next.

Exploring My Understanding

Complete the following sentence: To me, *dealing with disappointment* means . . .

Considering My Options

Complete the following sentence: NOW I'm going to . . .

UNLOCKING MY ANGER

Anger is an important emotion. Feeling anger signals the need to take action to protect our selves or others. We feel anger when our rights have been violated, when we've been treated with disrespect, when we're disappointed in others' actions, as well as our own, and when we're the target of or a witness to injustice.

Anger is an unacceptable emotion to many people because it isn't generally valued or accepted as an integral part of life's experience. Therefore we often suppress our anger. We tend to beat up on our selves and treat our selves with disrespect. We also tend to deny the existence of the anger because we're not supposed to feel that way about other people. When it can no longer be suppressed, an emotional explosion of anger is expressed (most often in inappropriate ways) and targeted at anyone who might get in the way at the time it occurs. Acts of domestic violence are often the result of pent-up anger that has no appropriate release.

The energy needed to avoid and suppress anger depletes our energy source. We're unable to accomplish our goals to the extent of our desires because our energy is tied up in holding on to the anger. Just as it's important for us to feel and express anger, it's also critical that we appropriately release it so that we can move ahead with our lives. Keep in mind people's actions don't *make* us angry; we must take ownership of how we respond to our emotions.

My Previous Experiences With Unlocking My Anger

Write down your experiences with unlocking your anger.

My Feelings About These Experiences

Write down your feelings about these experiences.

Suggested Exercises

1. When you feel anger, recognize your right to feel it. Refrain from taking any action while you're in the midst of the feeling. Remember that unchecked anger often brings out irrational behavior. When the potency of the anger has subsided, examine it. Ask your self:
    - How did this situation bring up these feelings?
    - What is my responsibility in the situation?
    - What can I do to positively contribute to the situation?

- How can I channel the energy from this anger into something positive?
- How can I let the other people know my feelings?

2. When you're feeling anger, it's your right and responsibility to let others involved in the situation with you know your feelings. A simple statement, such as, "I'm feeling very angry about what's going on here," conveys your feelings appropriately and lets others know your point-of-view. You may also want to comment on the reasons for your anger (if you know what they are) with a statement such as, "I feel my ideas are being devalued by the comments made by the group." Refrain from making accusatory remarks, such as "You make me so angry." When we accuse others, they usually become defensive and react in a negative way. Expressing your anger appropriately is challenging because your immediate urge is to act on your emotional response. Refrain from giving in to the urge.

3. You can release some of the energy associated with anger through physical activity. If you're particularly angered by a certain individual and you play a racquet sport, write his or her name on the balls. Then practice your most powerful shots on a backboard or against the wall. This physical activity releases pent-up anger and gives you a good physical workout as well.

4. Using visualization, close your eyes and picture your anger in your mind. Create a symbol for your anger. Blow up your anger as if it were a balloon. Make it as large as you possibly can. Then, letting the air out of your "anger balloon," shrink it down to the size of a pinpoint. Now, take an eraser and erase the point. This is a symbolic way to release your anger. It's a technique that benefits you and doesn't violate other's rights.

Exploring My Understanding

Complete the following sentence: To me, *unlocking my anger* means . . .

Considering My Options

Complete the following sentence: NOW I'm going to . . .

ADDRESSING MY NEEDS

Every human being has needs: physiological and psychological requirements for his or her well-being. There are certain needs that are naturally inherent in being human. As children it was the responsibility of our parents (or those acting in the role of parents) to meet those needs.

We still have needs that require our attention today. We have physiological needs. We have a need to feel safe and secure in our place in life. Because we are social beings, we have a need for social interactions and relationships. We have a need to feel positive about our selves. We have a need to stimulate our senses and our mental function. We have the need to express our thoughts, feelings and opinions. We have a need to give to others without expecting to receive something in return. We have a need to be whatever we want to be. We have a need to seek out the meaning of life.

As adults, we often forget that it's now our responsibility to meet our needs. No longer can we depend on others. If we wait for others to address our needs, it's likely they will go unmet.

My Previous Experiences With Addressing My Needs

Write down your experiences with addressing your needs.

My Feelings About These Experiences

Write down your feelings about these experiences.

Suggested Exercise

Draw a line down the middle of a sheet of paper. On the left side of the page, write down your needs as you define them, leaving space between them. On the right side of the page, write down how that need is currently being met and to what extent you are satisfied with what you're doing. As you review your findings, identify those needs that require more attention. Make a plan to address them more fully. If you have several, you may want to start with one and give it your full attention before addressing the others. Make a commitment to your self to be consciously aware of your needs so they can be satisfied.

Exploring My Understanding

Complete the following sentence: To me, *addressing my needs* means . . .

Considering My Options

Complete the following sentence: NOW I'm going to . . .

ACKNOWLEDGING MY DESIRES

If you could have anything you wanted, what would it be? If you could be your ideal, what would you be? You have the right and freedom to want anything. No desire is out of the realm of possibility.

We have desires for things or experiences because we expect to receive pleasure and satisfaction from attaining them. Desire is a natural outgrowth of the willingness to stretch and move beyond where we are right now. In desire, we find the seeds for developing strategies to pursue the goals we've set for our selves. When we feel ardent desire, we are passionate about our selves. That passion gives us the emotional energy to find ways to make our desires reality.

My Previous Experiences With Acknowledging My Desires

Write down your experiences with acknowledging your desires.

My Feelings About These Experiences

Write down your feelings about these experiences.

Suggested Exercise

You'll need several sheets of paper. On each page, put the general category of your desire in the center. Some categories could include places to visit, personal property, family, people, experiences, financial aspirations and education. Decide your own categories and be sure to use a lot of color in your work. (Color stimulates the brain's activity.) Now, on each page, write down, draw or symbolize whatever it is that you desire in that category. Keep these pages handy so you look at them often and add to them as new desires emerge. You may want to post them for easy access. Remind your self that you can desire anything you want.

Exploring My Understanding

Complete the following sentence: To me, *acknowledging my desires* means . . .

Considering My Options

Complete the following sentence: NOW I'm going to . . .

EXERCISING MY FREEDOM

"That's not what you saw." "You weren't listening to me—that's not what I said." "You shouldn't feel that way." "You could never be an artist. You're not that good." "Where on earth did you get that idea?" "How can you think that?" "You don't really want that, do you?"

Throughout our lives, we've been denied the freedom to feel, think, do, want and be what we wanted. In reality, you have complete freedom to feel, think, want and be. There is no penalty for thinking less than noble thoughts. There's no shame in wanting a better or different life. There's no limitation to what you can accomplish.

With freedom comes responsibility. You are responsible for your actions. You can think whatever you want to think. However, once you make your thoughts and feelings public information, you must deal with the consequences. With every action comes a consequence. For instance, you may wish someone would jump off a cliff because you're upset with him or her. If you convey this directly to the person, then you'll have to deal with their reaction.

Keep in mind that you have complete freedom in your life as long as you don't interfere with the freedom of others. Freedom and responsibility are inseparable.

My Previous Experiences With Exercising My Freedom

Write down your experiences with exercising your freedom.

My Feelings About These Experiences

Write down your feelings about these experiences.

Suggested Exercises

Read the book *Free to Be . . . You and Me* by Marlo Thomas. As you read the poems and stories, think about how the message of each one applies to your life.

Exploring My Understanding

Complete the following sentence: To me, *exercising my freedom* means . . .

Considering My Options

Complete the following sentence: NOW I'm going to . . .

NURTURING AND TREATING MY SELF ESPECIALLY NICE

Nurturing is something that we learn about through experience and role models in our lives. We depend on others for nurturing when we are children. When we become adults, the responsibility becomes ours.

We tend to believe that the act of nurturing takes at least two people. Although we may enjoy nurturing relationships with others, we cannot solely depend on them to provide and care for us. We have a responsibility to nurture our selves. The experience of being nurtured is vital to having a full and rewarding life.

To nurture means to cherish, nourish, care for, provide for, foster and further the development of your self or another. Are you being nurtured? When you are, you're reminded of your value, your uniqueness and your worth. When you engage in nurturing behaviors, you're treating your self with dignity and respect. You're treating your self especially nice. Nurturance gives us energy, encouragement and confidence.

We take pleasure in doing nice things for others. We delight in watching a loved one open a card or a gift. We give gift certificates. We send flowers to let others know we care about and love them.

We typically don't take these courses of action for our selves. We expect others to do nice things for us and we wait until they do. When our expectations are not met, we're disappointed.

We often feel we don't deserve nice treats for our selves. Just as we give to others we also need to give to our selves. When we treat our selves well, we're more likely to treat others well, too. You deserve to be nurtured.

You deserve to be pampered. You deserve special treats. Don't wait on someone else to read your mind. You could be waiting a long time, and you'd be denying your self simple pleasures in life.

My Previous Experiences With Nurturing And Treating My Self Especially Nice

Write down your experiences with nurturing your self.

My Feelings About These Experiences

Write down your feelings about these experiences.

Suggested Exercises

1. Think about how you feel when you are nurtured. Make a list of ways you enjoy being cared for by others. Then identify how you currently care for your self. Consider other things you can do to provide for your needs as well as further the development of your quest for getting what you want out of life. Finally, make a commitment to your self to engage in a nurturing activity every day—even if only for a few minutes.

2. Think of that special something that you really enjoy receiving from others. Then give your self that gift. For example, if you enjoy receiving flowers, have an arrangement delivered to you from an anonymous admirer (especially if the people in your office are particularly interested in your affairs). If you want to go to a special concert and no one has invited you to go, buy your self a ticket and go anyway.

3. Treat your self to a full body massage or a manicure and pedicure or a long afternoon walk in the park or some uninterrupted time listening to your favorite music. Do whatever is a special treat for you. Don't wait for someone else. If you want, you can always invite someone else to join you in your adventures, but having someone else around isn't necessary.

Exploring My Understanding

Complete the following sentence: To me, *nurturing and treating my self especially nice* means . . .

Considering My Options

Complete the following sentence: NOW I'm going to . . .

FEELING GOOD ABOUT BEING ME

How you feel about your self is reflected in everything you do as well as in your relationships with your self and others. When you feel good about being you, then your perspective about life in general and your ideas about other people are more positive. The same holds true if you feel lousy about your self, then you'll also tend to feel lousy about life and others.

When you feel positive about your self, you don't feel a need to put others down so you'll *look* good. Neither do you feel a need to compare your self with others, measuring what you perceive to be your shortcomings against what others seem to have going for them.

Feeling good about being you means celebrating your individuality, value, talents, skills, abilities and gifts for giving what you have to others. When you feel good about being your self, you also have the confidence to make whatever changes you want in life. You have the strength to grow and move forward to get whatever it is you want. You realize that you are being your best even when your *best* may fall short of someone else's or your own expectations.

My Previous Experiences With Feeling Good About Me

Write down your experiences with feeling good about being you.

My Feelings About These Experiences

Write down your feelings about these experiences.

Suggested Exercises

1. Take a very big poster board or paper and on it write "I, (your name), feel great about being me!" in big, bold colorful letters. Affix to the surface a recent picture of your self that you particularly like. Then draw, write or create a way to post your reasons for feeling good about being your self. Attach this to a wall, a door, or another conspicuous place so you can see it and add to it as you think of more reasons. Use colorful markers or paint to record your information. This can be a perpetual project or you can use it when you're feeling down to remind your self of the many reasons to feel good about your self.

2. Begin your day, by stating 10 reasons you feel good about being your self. Say to your self out loud, "I'm feeling good about me because . . ." then finish the sentence with something positive about your self. Use "I'm feeling . . ." at the beginning of each statement. You can do this exercise anytime during the day or

evening. It comes in handy especially when you're feeling a little low. You can vary this exercise by writing your responses.

Exploring My Understanding

Complete the following sentence: To me, *feeling good about being me* means . . .

Considering My Options

Complete the following sentence: NOW I'm going to . . .

TALKING TO MY SELF

We talk to our selves constantly. We give our selves encouragement, build confidence, evaluate performances and give feedback. With our talk, we engage in building or destroying our self-esteem.

Each of us has an endless tape loop that plays continuously. The recordings on this tape first appeared when we were born. Various people who have been influential in our lives have made contributions to our tapes. Those influential people include our parents, relatives, friends, teachers, spouses and children—anyone we've had an emotional connection with. We hold onto these messages as if they are truth. We act and respond based on the content of the messages on our tapes.

The best way to determine what's on your tape is to pay

attention to what you say to your self when you make a mistake. You may have recordings of "You stupid idiot! How could you be so dumb!" or "Where did you get the bright idea that you'd be able to find the answer to this problem?" or "I can't believe what kind of fool I've raised!"

Often we say things to our selves that we really wouldn't want to repeat to another human being nor would we direct those same comments to someone else. And we'd get really angry is someone made those comments to us. Yet, we continually beat our selves up because we fail to meet expectations.

What we say to our selves is extremely powerful. Our brains register the comments, positive and negative, each time they are made. And both sides of our brain believe what they hear. It's up to you to change the tape. It's up to you to make encouraging and supportive comments to your self.

My Previous Experiences With Talking To My Self

Write down your experiences with talking to your self.

My Feelings About These Experiences

Write down your feelings about these experiences.

Suggested Exercises

1. For a day, write down everything you say to your self. If it's a supportive, self-esteem building statement, mark

it with an "S". If it's a destructive statement, mark it with a "D". Then look at your "D" statements. How can you rephrase the statements so they will communicate support and encouragement? If you need some assistance, look at your "S" statements, listen to others commend others, and ask people you respect what they say to themselves for perseverance and encouragement.

2. When you talk to your self, you want to remember that your conversation has three components: words, emotions and pictures. You want your words to be personal (using "I," "me," and "my"), positive (using what you are, not what you're not) and in the present tense ("I am an effective decision maker"), even if you really don't feel that way at first. Attach powerful emotions to your words. Say your statements with conviction and enthusiasm, even if it's a challenge for you to do so. Remember it's the emotion that carries the message to the brain and imprints it on the audio tape. Using visualization, picture your self doing whatever it is you want to do effectively or saying whatever it is you want to say articulately. By using images, you're practicing for the next time you find your self in a similar situation. When you create your image, remember to feel the confidence you'll need when you deal with this situation in reality. If you hear your self say something negative, immediately rephrase the statement in positive terms. Practice makes permanent.

Exploring My Understanding

Complete the following sentence: To me, *talking to my self* means . . .

Considering My Options

Complete the following sentence: NOW I'm going to . . .

CELEBRATING MY UNIQUENESS

There is no one in this world just like you. You are a unique composite of emotions, talents, abilities, desires, intellect, intuition, motivation and strength. No one sees the world the same way you do or has the same experiences you do or feels exactly how you do. Even if you're a twin, raised by the same parents in the same home, you are unique.

Too often we want to be like everybody else. We want to keep up with the Joneses. We want to wear the same clothes. We want to spend our time the same way that we perceive everyone else does. Even if we behave similarly on the outside, there's still a uniqueness within our selves that can't be denied.

Look for ways you can use your uniqueness to help others, promote growth in society, and further your own development. Celebrate the contribution your difference makes.

My Previous Experiences With Celebrating My Uniqueness

Write down your experiences with celebrating your uniqueness.

My Feelings About These Experiences

Write down your feelings about these experiences.

Suggested Exercise

You'll need to solicit the help of one of your closest friends for this exercise. Let him or her know that you're in the process of expanding your knowledge about your self and need some help. Ask your friend to write you a letter detailing your unique attributes, what makes you special, and why you're important to him or her. Let your friend know that this is a part of the process of celebrating your uniqueness. Once you receive the letter, promptly thank your friend for using his or her time, energy and resources to help you in your endeavor. Then take some time to read the letter, looking at the perspective shared with you. Compare your thoughts about your self with those of your friend. Then celebrate your uniqueness in whatever way works for you. (It takes guts to ask someone to do this for you. Your true friends will help you!)

Exploring My Understanding

Complete the following sentence: To me, *celebrating my uniqueness* means . . .

Considering My Options

Complete the following sentence: NOW I'm going to . . .

COMMENDING MY SELF

As human beings we like to be acknowledged for the accomplishments we achieve in life. When we reach one of life's many milestones, such as graduating from school, moving into a new home, getting married or having children, we let others know about it and enjoy receiving the gifts they give us in celebration of that accomplishment. We enjoy the recognition we receive for stretching beyond our limits, for moving out of our comfort zones.

Somewhere we learned that it's appropriate for others to commend us, say positive things, give us gifts, hugs, and well-deserved pats on the back. Yet, the art of commending our selves is foreign to most of us. We don't feel we have permission to celebrate the small steps we take toward our goals or even the greater, more visible accomplishments we attain.

If you think about it, you'll realize you're really the best person to commend your self. You're the only one who truly knows what kind of investment of your time, energy and resources you've made. When you get into the habit of commending your self, you'll find what others say, think and do won't be as necessary for you to move on to your next challenge.

My Previous Experiences With Commending My Self

Write down your experiences with commending your self.

My Feelings About These Experiences

Write down your feelings about these experiences.

Suggested Exercise

1. Think about the last time you were commended by someone else for something you accomplished. How did you feel about that person? How did you feel about your self?

2. Think about the last time *you commended your self* for something you accomplished. How did you feel about your self? How did you feel about commending your self?

3. If the act of commending your self seems foreign to you, try this: In your mind, picture an accomplishment you experienced. Make the scene very vivid, filling it up with colors, sounds, tastes, smells and the feelings you experienced. Listen to the words others were saying to you about how proud they were of you. Now hear your self saying words of encouragement and praise to your self. Tell your self how proud you are of your efforts and accomplishment. Feel the pride that comes from hearing these comments. You may want to do this exercise several times, using different accomplishments until you feel comfortable with commending your self.

4. Make a list of ways you enjoy commending your self. Your list could include phrases you'd say to your self, a new CD, a massage, a trip, quiet time. (It is strongly recommended that food items not be included on your list. Save food for nourishing your body—to eat when you're truly hungry!) Select whatever works for you. If you're not sure what you'd like to put on your list,

experiment. Then when you experience success, whether it be great or small, make a selection from your list and enjoy. In reality, commending yourself for the smaller successes is more important than doing so for the larger ones. The more frequent commendations will not only give you recognition for the steps you're making toward your accomplishments, it will also give you encouragement to persevere! Besides, others generally commend you for the big stuff.

Exploring My Understanding

Complete the following sentence: To me *commending my self* means . . .

Considering My Options

Complete the following sentence: NOW I'm going to . . .

MOVING OUT OF MY COMFORT ZONE

We like to feel comfortable. We seek it out. We like to know what to expect. We like to be able to predict what's going to happen as a result of our actions. Inconvenient surprises are a nuisance to us. We want to feel in control of every situation. As long as we linger in the comfort zone, our awareness and willingness to entertain fresh new ideas will be limited. Our horizons will be narrowed rather than broadened.

In order to grow and fully experience life, we must risk new experiences that lead to new perspectives. It's only when we're willing to take those risks that we learn and experience life anew over and over again. Otherwise we tend to have the same experience repeatedly with nothing ever changing. To get what you want in life requires that you move out of your comfort zone. It requires becoming comfortable with being uncomfortable. What you desire won't come to you unless you go out to meet it.

My Previous Experiences With Moving Out Of My Comfort Zone

Write down your experiences with moving out of your comfort zone.

My Feelings About These Experiences

Write down your feelings about these experiences.

Suggested Exercise

To experience moving out of your comfort zone, do things you're use to doing differently and do things you've never done. Here is a list of suggestions:

- Attend an ethnic celebration.
- Take a trip to an unknown destination.

- Learn a new skill.
- Wear clothes that don't match.
- Wear pink socks instead of white ones.
- Brush your teeth with a different hand.
- Tell someone how you really feel about him or her.
- Go home from work a different way. (Not recommended for going to work—you don't want to be late!)
- Go white water rafting.
- Take an elderly person out to lunch.
- Keep your neighbor's pet for a week.
- Volunteer your time to a community project.
- Sample foods unfamiliar to you.
- Learn a new language.

Add to the list as you enjoy moving out of your comfort zone. Share your experiences with others. Your stories will give them courage to move out of their comfort zones, too!

Exploring My Understanding

Complete the following sentence: To me, *moving out of my comfort zone* means . . .

Considering My Options

Complete the following sentence: NOW I'm going to . . .

SPENDING TIME ALONE

Most of our waking hours are spent with others, interacting directly or indirectly. We find that any time we do have to our selves is cherished because of its rarity.

Yet, some of us actually prefer the busyness because it gives us an excuse for not taking the time to get to know the real person inside of our selves.

Spending time alone is beneficial because it gives us the opportunity to get to know our selves better—to become better acquainted with our wants, needs and goals. Time alone gives us the opportunity to nurture our selves, to treat our selves in a special way and to fill our selves up so we'll have more to give to others. It's a time when we can relax and put aside the cares of the day for just a few minutes. The benefit you'll experience from spending time alone on a regular basis is far-reaching, positively affecting the elements in each dimension of life.

My Previous Experiences With Spending Time Alone

Write down your experiences with spending time alone.

My Feelings About These Experiences

Write down your feelings about these experiences.

Suggested Exercise

To begin with, set aside at least 15 minutes a day for your self. (You'll likely want to increase the amount of time you spend with your self once you've experienced the benefits.) You may want to get up 15 minutes earlier than everyone else or you may want to stay up 15 minutes later in the evenings. You can also consider taking time for your self between work and home. What you do with this time is entirely up to you. You may choose to meditate, relax, walk, read poetry, listen to music, reflect on your progress toward a goal or sit quietly. Keep in mind this is time you've set aside for your self for getting to know your self better, for nurturing and for replenishing your energies.

Exploring My Understanding

Complete the following sentence: To me, *spending time alone* means . . .

Considering My Options

Complete the following sentence: NOW I'm going to . . .

TAKING TIME TO REFLECT

We live in a very fast-paced society. We spend so much time *doing* that we rarely take the time to reflect on our growth, accomplishments, learning and the progress we're making in pursuit of our goals. Some people avoid reflection because it can be painful to realize that what you learn is contrary to what you believe or want.

Reflection serves a powerful purpose. It gives us an opportunity to determine if the track we're on is taking us where we want to go. Reflection gives us time to evaluate how our efforts are contributing to our well-being and the well-being of those we love. It allows us to examine our actions and attitudes. Reflection calls for taking a critical look at how we spend our time, energy and resources. It enables us to clear our thinking about situations that may be causing us some concern.

Getting away from the hustle and bustle of life is necessary for the reflection process. Finding a place that is peaceful, calm and conducive to thinking is strongly recommended. Reflection is a critical element for moving ahead in life and getting what you want.

My Previous Experiences With Taking Time To Reflect

Write down your experiences with taking time to reflect.

My Feelings About These Experiences

Write down your feelings about these experiences.

Suggested Exercise

Set aside an hour or two each week to spend time in a natural surrounding, such as a park, garden, river, beach, stream, mountains. You may want to walk while you're reflecting or you may want to find a comfortable place to sit or recline. During this time, think about how your life and how your week unfolded. Use the following questions to guide your reflection:

- Did you accomplish what you intended to do?
- Did you move closer to attaining your goals?
- Did you handle situations in an effective way?
- Did you treat others with dignity and respect?
- Did you treat your self with dignity and respect?
- Did you take time for play?
- Did you spend time with people who are important to you?
- What were the highlights of the week?
- What lessons did you learn?
- What new talent did you uncover?
- What will you do differently in the coming week to make it work better for you?

With the answers you receive, plan for any changes you might want to make in your upcoming week. (Although taking time to reflect as described here is typically an individual process, it's one that could be beneficial for couples, too.)

Exploring My Understanding

Complete the following sentence: To me, *taking time to reflect* means . . .

Considering My Options

Complete the following sentence: NOW I'm going to . . .

GETTING AWAY FROM IT ALL

True vacation time has become an anomaly. Working vacations have become the norm. You may feel you can't get away for even an overnight trip. You may tell your self, "There's just too much to do! I'm behind already. If I go away, I'll never get caught up!" In reality, if you never get away, if you never "retreat," you won't have the energy to keep going at your rat-race pace. You'll eventually burn out leaving your self with an empty sense of accomplishment.

Taking a vacation, getting away, or going on a retreat helps you nourish your sense of self. This renewal helps you regain a clear perspective about who you are and how you're fulfilling your purpose in life. Getting away from the everyday routine gives you opportunities to consider where you are in relation to where you want to be with your life. Retreating helps you to envision what's in store for you. Getting away helps you relax and just be with your self.

My Previous Experiences With Getting Away From It All

Write down your experiences with getting away from it all.

My Feelings About These Experiences

Write down your feelings about these experiences.

Suggested Exercise

Plan to take a minimum of four trips a year, one each quarter. Vary the length if you like, making some long weekends and others extended stays. Go to places you enjoy, where you can truly relax. Leave your work at work. DO NOT CALL THE OFFICE. Do away with schedules and fixed agendas. Feel free to do absolutely nothing. Consider taking at least one trip by your self so you'll have an opportunity to reflect, renew and relax on a very personal level.

Exploring My Understanding

Complete the following sentence: To me, *getting away from it all* means . . .

Considering My Options

Complete the following sentence: NOW I'm going to . . .

6
Growing InSync with the Mental Dimension

It is through the conscious and unconscious thought processes of the mental dimension that we make sense out of our beingness. Through the power of our brains we become aware of our spirituality, interpret our existence, experience our emotions, define our relationships and control our bodily functions and activities. Our minds constantly monitor our thoughts, feelings and actions and communicate their presence, their viability and their importance to us. When the mental dimension is out of sync, we have no way of knowing about our experiences, about our selves or about others. Our thoughts provide the foundation for understanding this experience we call life.

The interconnectedness in our lives demands balance within the dimensions so that our minds can be clear to make effective decisions that will bring benefit to us. If we are emotionally distraught or over-involved with our emotionality, the cognitive processes are negatively affected. They're unable to work for us because the emotional dimension is overloading our system. How we attend to the needs of our physical dimension affects how effectively the brain works. Lack of physical exercise and rest clouds our thought processes. Exercise moves oxygen throughout the brain which it needs to function properly. If we feed our bodies toxic substances or our bodily systems don't function well, then the brain's ability to function properly is negatively affected. We need to balance the mental with respect to the other dimensions because too much rational thought about one's life or excessive analysis about one's place on this earth can interfere with the enjoyment of life.

The power of your brain offers you the opportunities to acquire the knowledge and skills that enable you to make conscious choices about your life. Exercises that will benefit you as you pursue your own direction and fulfill your purpose include establishing priorities; setting, pursuing and abandoning goals; and maximizing the use of your time, energy and resources. Understanding your view of the world, resolving internal conflict and dealing with challenges will also be explored. You'll learn to enhance your creativity, energize the power of the brain, organize your life, and learn through your experiences.

Please refer to page 40 for directions on how to maximize your experiences.

MAKING MY DREAMS REALITY

We have many dreams throughout our lifetimes. As youngsters we dream of being astronauts, fire fighters, truck drivers and rock stars. Some of us have such emotional involvement in our dreams that we willingly and relentlessly pursue them until they become reality. Too often most of us ignore, release or deny our dreams rather than pursue them. Many of us feel we don't deserve to have what we want because we've been told we're not good enough. Our dreams can become reality if we believe in our selves and are willing to put forth the effort to get what we want.

In order to make your dreams real, you must first dream. If you choose not to dream, then life will be mundane without stimulation and enthusiasm. Dreams give us energy and motivation to move ahead and realize we can have anything we want. It's true that some people perceive dreams as an avoidance technique, or a way to escape reality. Yet, dreams can enrich your reality if you're willing to let go of your inhibitions and let your mind explore the very depths of your being.

My Previous Experiences With Making My Dreams Reality

Write down your experiences with making your dreams reality.

My Feelings About These Experiences

Write down your feelings about these experiences.

Suggested Exercise

Set aside some time to daydream. You may want to be surrounded by nature or find a particularly quiet place. Ask your self, "If I could be anything I want to be, what would I be?" and "If I could have anything I want, what would I have?" Then let your creative juices flow and your mind explore the possibilities. When you have an idea that's of particular interest to you, take a few moments to create a full color picture using all of your senses to elaborate. Then let your emotions flow. Feel how you'd feel if this dream was in fact your reality. Once you've found a dream that fires you up and fills you with passion, decide if you want to set a goal to make it really happen. You may want to review the dream several times, but then move on!

Exploring My Understanding

Complete the following sentence: To me, *making my dreams reality* means . . .

Considering My Options

Complete the following sentence: NOW I'm going to . . .

SETTING GOALS

One of the most effective ways to get what you truly want out of life is to set goals. By setting goals, you take responsibility for the direction your life will take. You don't leave your happiness or your place in life to chance. Although dreams and wishes are valuable unto themselves, transforming them into definite goals will allow them to become reality.

Having goals in place gives you direction as well as purpose. Goals enable you to maximize the use of your time, energy and resources. In order for goals to work, they must be meaningful. They need to be clearly and positively stated in the present tense (as if you had already reached the goal). They need to be time sensitive as you assess your progress toward the goals and to determine if you want to continue pursuing them. Most importantly, you must feel an emotional involvement with the goals AND the goals must be in writing. When we write our goals, we're making a commitment to our selves and to achieving what we want. You can benefit from having goals for all areas of your life: mental, social, spiritual, emotional, physical and career/financial.

If you are not currently a goal setter, you may want to begin this process in one area. Plunging into all six areas as a first experience would be overwhelming. If you set a goal to develop or improve an area in your physical dimension, know that your other dimensions will benefit, too. Once you become accustomed to working with goals, you can extend your efforts to the other dimensions in your life.

My Previous Experiences With Setting Goals

Write down your experiences with setting goals.

My Feelings About These Experiences

Write down your feelings about these experiences.

Suggested Exercise

Use the following process to select new goals that you want to pursue:

Write your goal in detail.
Then answer the following questions about your goal.

1. Do I really want this?
2. Do I believe I have at least a 50/50 chance of reaching this goal?
3. Is my goal written in detail?
4. How will I benefit from reaching this goal?
5. Where am I in relation to my goal right now?
6. What is my time frame for reaching this goal?
7. What obstacles (including people) will get in my way?
8. What is my plan for eliminating the obstacles?
9. What do I need to learn in order to reach this goal?
10. Who are the people who can help me reach this goal?
11. What is my detailed plan (include activities that are sequenced)?
12. How will I monitor my progress?
13. What will I do to commend myself?
14. Will I give up when the going gets tough?

Exploring My Understanding

Complete the following sentence: To me, *setting goals* means . . .

Considering My Options

Complete the following sentence: NOW I'm going to . . .

PURSUING GOALS

The value of setting and reaching goals is found in the process of pursuing them. The benefits we receive come from the experiences we have and the lessons we learn while striving to make our goals become reality.

It's erroneous to believe that once you've set the goal that all you have to do is wait. Setting the goal is just the beginning. Once you've focused your desires and written your goal in action-oriented terms, then the process of getting what you want begins. To make your goal become reality you must work on your detailed plan. Often we get caught up in just getting to the goal. Our tunnel vision interferes with our ability to enjoy life and see the opportunities that arise that could help us move closer to our goal. We often ignore the lessons that are inherent in the process.

Although the goals you set are very clear to you, it's critical to be willing to make modifications as you go along. You're probably not the same person you were when you established the goal, so you may want to make some changes. Being flexible as well as relaxed will greatly benefit the process. Most goals require a sequence of activities, and part of the pursuit is monitoring your progress in completing them.

My Previous Experiences With Pursuing Goals

Write down your experiences with pursuing your goals.

My Feelings About These Experiences

Write down your feelings about these experiences.

Suggested Exercise

One way to monitor the progress you're making toward your goal is to make a grid. At the top of your page, write your goal. On the left side, write the activities in a sequence that you need to complete. At the top of each column write in target dates. On a regular basis (daily or weekly), review the goal and the activities to determine how you are progressing. If you're not moving as quickly as you would like to, look at your barriers and determine what you will need to do about them.

Exploring My Understanding

Complete the following sentence: To me, *pursuing goals* means . . .

Considering My Options

Complete the following sentence: NOW I'm going to . . .

ABANDONING GOALS

You may find it strange to have this idea and exercise included in a book that's a guide on how to get what you want in life, but it's important to know that you can let go of goals that you no longer wish to pursue.

As we change, so do our desires. A goal that you ardently desired last year may no longer hold the emotional charge it did at that time. Your circumstances and direction in life may change. Abandoning a goal is a smart thing to do if it is no longer consistent with the direction your life has taken.

If you pursue your goal without passion, your time, energy and resources will be depleted and you will not have the strength to pursue those things you really want.

You may think that people who abandon their goals may be wishy-washy or don't know how to persevere. There's no stigma or disgrace in letting go of a goal that no longer has any benefits for you. Release the old goals with joy, and then you'll have the freedom to replace them with new ones that bring you pleasure and satisfaction.

My Previous Experiences With Abandoning Goals

Write down your experiences with abandoning your goals.

My Feelings About These Experiences

Write down your feelings about these experiences.

Suggested Exercise

Take a look at your current goals. Examine each one of them carefully. Determine if you continue to be emotionally committed to the goal. Also affirm that this goal is one you want, not one that someone else wants for you. If you find any goals that you no longer really desire or that someone else has selected for you, remove them from your goal list. You'll have more time, energy and resources to invest in the goals that continue to be viable.

Exploring My Understanding

Complete the following sentence: To me, *abandoning goals* means . . .

Considering My Options

Complete the following sentence: NOW I'm going to . . .

ESTABLISHING PRIORITIES

What does your list of priorities look like? Who or what is at the top? Priorities are people, things and activities that are important to us. It's beneficial to be clear about what's important. This clarity helps you maximize the expenditure of your time, energy and resources.

Knowing what's important helps you make conscious choices about what you want to do with your life. There are times when you have competing priorities. When two people or activities are both important to you, you must choose. You need to evaluate your emotional involvement and the subsequent benefit(s) you'll receive from the choice you make.

How do you decide on your number one priority? Without a doubt, the most important person in your life is YOU. Everyone benefits when you make your self the number one priority. When you take care of your self, you have so much more to give others. It's quite difficult to invest in others without first investing in your self. When you do an effective job of taking care of your self, you'll be in a much better position to expend your time, energy and resources on other people and activities from your list of priorities.

Establishing and attending to your priorities is an effective way to get what you want in life as well as helping others achieve their goals.

My Previous Experiences With Establishing Priorities

Write down your experiences with establishing priorities.

My Feelings About These Experiences

Write down your feelings about these experiences.

Suggested Exercise

Make a list of your priorities. Number them in order of importance. (My suggestion is YOU are number one!) Examine your reasons for the order you chose. Determine if you need to make any changes in your priorities. Once you're satisfied with your choices, write your priorities on cards and put them in conspicuous places. At the bottom of each card, write this question: *Does what I'm doing right now support my priorities?* Refer to the cards frequently to verify that you're engaged in activities that are important to you.

Exploring My Understanding

Complete the following sentence: To me, *establishing priorities* means . . .

Considering My Options

Complete the following sentence: NOW I'm going to . . .

MANAGING MY TIME, ENERGY AND RESOURCES

This moment is the most important moment of your life. You have no guarantee of the next. Regardless of social class, ethnicity, religion, nationality and all other individual differences, each of us is given the gift of 24 hours in a day—moment by moment. No amount of influence, power or money can change that reality. Time passes without regard to any external circumstance—time truly moves to the beat of its own drum.

How we choose to use our time makes a significant difference in our lives. The level of energy we enjoy depends on a number of factors, including how we rest, relax and nourish our bodies, our basic genetic make-up and metabolism rate and how enthusiastic we are about life. Resources include our talents and skills, the ability to use our creative and intellectual capabilities, the ability to stimulate others to move into action as well as money and financial assets.

Time, energy and resources are valuable commodities. If we don't deliberately make choices about how we're going to use them, at the end of the day we'll find that they were spent on inconsequential activities or that others used them for their own benefit.

When you consider how you spend your time, expend your energy and allocate your resources, make certain to include goal-oriented activities and priorities. Keep in mind that there are everyday responsibilities (things required of us that are not particularly goal or priority related) as well as mind-body-spirit maintenance activities (like taking a shower, eating meals, personal grooming, resting and relaxing) that require your attention, too.

You have a choice. You can let time, energy and resources pass you by, or you can consciously choose how to effectively use them by focusing on your goals and priorities—by doing what's important. Time, energy and resources are gifts. Find ways to maximize their use and effectiveness.

My Previous Experiences With Managing Time, Energy And Resources

Write down your experiences with managing time, energy and resources.

My Feelings About These Experiences

Write down your feelings about these experiences.

Suggested Exercises

1. Keep a detailed record of how you spend your time for at least a day. At day's end, code your activities. Mark goal-related activities with a **G**. Mark priority-oriented activities with a **P**. Mark responsibilities with an **R**. And mark maintenance-oriented activities with an **M**. Examine your findings. Where are you spending your time, energy and resources? Are you satisfied? If not then consciously decide to make whatever changes necessary to maximize the use of your time, energy and resources.

2. To manage your time more effectively, use these five tools for planning and scheduling your days:

   a. You need to maintain *one calendar* on which you record *all* of your appointments (personal and work-related). By maintaining one calendar you won't miss important meetings with your clients, your family, your friends or your self. (You may also want to keep a common calendar in a central place in your home if you're coordinating schedules with others.)

   b. You'll want to establish a *routine* of planning your day, week, month and year. Set aside a time each day for planning. Some people prefer to plan at the end of the day, while others prefer to plan first thing in the morning. Find a time that works for you and stick to it. It's also recommended that you spend some time at the beginning of each month and each week to get an overview of what's ahead. By looking at the broader picture, you'll be able to group common tasks and activities, as well as prioritize what needs to be done.

c. Designate a *place* where you'll do your planning for the next day. Getting your self into the routine of sitting down to plan in a particular place will make it easier to develop the habit of planning.

d. Use a *To Do List* of the tasks that you want to complete. Prioritize your list so you'll be sure to complete the most important tasks. Ask your self, *how important is it for me to do this? Can I delegate this task to someone else? Does this task need to be completed at all? What is the most important use of my time today? Does what I'm doing support my goals and priorities? Will my doing this task matter in 10 years?* Make a commitment to your self to do only the important things.

e. When planning your day, have your *written goals* available as a reference. You'll want to include goal-directed activities each day when possible.

Exploring My Understanding

Complete the following sentence: To me, *managing time, energy and resources* means . . .

Considering My Options

Complete the following sentence: NOW I'm going to . . .

SAYING "NO" WHEN I NEED TO

Saying "no" even when we want to is hard because we like helping others. We like to be perceived by others as being helpful. We're not sure we have a right to say "no." We're often concerned that being unwilling or unable to help another will have negative consequences for us later. We may think "If I tell him 'no' now then he might not . . . for me." We're always concerned with maintaining a balance between giving and receiving. We may even verbalize, "Since you helped me out on my project, I'll help you out on yours."

While there is merit in helping others, it's equally important to give other people the opportunity to help one another. Others often approach us with, "Nobody else can do this the way you can," and they are absolutely right. Others can bring a fresh perspective to the community project, and they will also benefit through their giving. So if you choose not to help, there will be someone else who can.

Too often we don't put a limit on what we give away. We don't like to admit we're not indispensable. Yet, saying "yes" without conscious thought will deter us from the path we're creating for our selves unless helping others get what they want will also help us get what we want. There are indeed appropriate times to say "yes." Just make sure you're making a conscious choice to do so.

My Previous Experiences With Saying "No" When I Need To

Write down your experiences with saying "no" when you need to.

My Feelings About These Experiences

Write down your feelings about these experiences.

Suggested Exercise

When someone asks you to do something, use the following procedure to respond:

1. Thank them for asking you. Tell them you want to think about their request and that you'll let them know by a specified time.
2. Compare the request for the use of your time, energy and resources with *your* goals and priorities. If there is a match, then you know your agreement to assist will contribute to what you want. If there isn't a match, then you know that to say "yes" to their request will not move you in the direction of your choice.
3. Give your response. If your response is "yes," then let them know the framework within which you can best work. If your response is "no," then an appropriate response would be something similar to "Thank you for asking me to . . . I've given your request much thought and have decided to say 'no'." (You may want to practice saying "no" several times before actually giving your response. Practice with a friend. Use visualization to build your confidence.)
4. Refrain from giving reasons or giving in to subtle and not-so-subtle pressure to change your mind. Remember you've made a conscious choice about what you want to do with your time, energy and resources. Stick to it!

Exploring My Understanding

Complete the following sentence: To me, *saying "no" when I need to* means . . .

Considering My Options

Complete the following sentence: NOW I'm going to . . .

ORGANIZING MY LIFE'S ACTIVITIES

Some people boast that they thrive in disorganized clutter, claiming that they work better at a messy desk or in a messy office, and that they can put their finger on whatever they need whenever they need it. In reality, they use up a lot of time searching.

One of the keys to organizing your life's activities is to create your own storage and retrieval system for the items in your home as well as in your office. When you have a system, you can retrieve and store quickly. Your system must be simple, easy to remember and make sense to you. Have a place for everything, such as tools, magazines, cleaning supplies, etc. When you finish using any item, return it to its place. The next time you need it, it'll be there waiting for you. For example, if you take pictures, put them in photo albums so you can enjoy and share them with others.

Create a filing system for your paper, such as bills, canceled checks, receipts, insurance information, warranties, etc., so that you can easily file and retrieve the information you need. Refrain from stacking paper. You'll waste a lot of time by going through stacks.

Take action on paper when you receive it. If you don't have time to respond to your mail, wait to open it until you do. Read your first class mail only—toss the junk mail! Keep important records and documents, such as wills, insurance policies, stock certificates, passports, in a safe place, such as a safety deposit box at a bank or a fireproof safe in your home.

Establish a routine for completing certain tasks. For example, perhaps you do your household chores on Tuesdays, pay your bills on Thursdays, and attend to your plants and garden on Saturday. The more routine you have in your life for those essential maintenance activities, the more time you'll have to do the things you really want to do.

Develop a system for cleaning out things you collect. Keeping things that are no longer useful clutter your environment and your life.

Having a systematic way to organize your environment and your possessions will eliminate a lot of frustration. Your brain works more efficiently as well as more effectively when you have less clutter in your environment. There is no true value to just having stuff. If you can't use it, someone else can. If it's broken and you're not going to fix it, throw it away. An organized environment is freeing. It gives you more time and energy to pursue what you really want in life.

My Previous Experiences With Organizing My Life's Activities

Write down your experiences with organizing your life's activities.

My Feelings About These Experiences

Write down your feelings about these experiences.

Suggested Exercise

Target one of your "collections" (clothes, magazines, greeting cards, old holiday gifts) that you have accumulated over the years. Set aside some time to purge the items that you no longer need or use. Determine what you can give or throw away. A good rule of thumb to decide if it's in your best interest to get rid of an item, is to determine if you have worn it or used it within the past year. If you haven't, the likelihood of using it in the future is close to nil. (This wouldn't apply to specialty items such as scuba equipment or gardening tools.) No doubt you will experience some emotionality and sentimentality about some of the items that you no longer use. Keep in mind what's important *now*.

Things that were important at one time can create more clutter than is healthy. Remember your goal is to be more organized and to rid your self and your environment of unnecessary clutter.

Exploring My Understanding

Complete the following sentence: To me, *organizing my life's activities* means . . .

Considering My Options

Complete the following sentence: NOW I'm going to . . .

UNDERSTANDING MY VIEW OF THE WORLD

Your view of the world is the result of your experiences, value system, biases and prejudices, ethnicity, level of education, regional or national origin, parental upbringing, relationships, language, religion, preferences, intellectual abilities and creative curiosities. Your view of the world differs from that of any other person. It's the foundation for your uniqueness. Every experience you have, everything you learn is filtered through your current view of the world. How you perceive any situation is based on how that situation relates to your understanding of life at that moment. Your perception affects your self-esteem, relationships and behavior. Your perception represents your reality. The meaning you attach to your reality is based on the value you place on that reality.

As you grow and develop, your reality changes. Your reality may not be congruent with the reality of those around you or even with your past reality. For example, think about how you perceived your world as a child, then as a teenager, then as an adult. Think about what seems different to you this year from last year. Because we're dynamic, ever changing human beings, our view of the world will continue to change as we do. Keep in mind that the more you understand your view of the world, the greater appreciation you'll have for others' views. Each one is distinctive and real.

My Previous Experiences With Understanding My View Of The World

Write down your experiences with understanding your view of the world.

My Feelings About These Experiences

Write down your feelings about this experience.

Suggested Exercises

Find a picture—any type will do—and look at it for no more than five minutes. Then put the picture away and write down everything you observed, felt and thought about it. Put your dated notes away along with the picture. Allow at least three weeks to elapse before you look at the picture again. DO NOT LOOK AT YOUR PREVIOUS NOTES. After looking at the picture again for no more than five minutes, put it away and follow the same procedure. Be sure you date your notes. Do this exercise several times (at least four) before you compare your notes. When you're ready to compare notes, look for similarities as well as differences. If you see changes from time to time, you have evidence of change in your view of the world. You're seeing the picture with different eyes. If your notes are identical, then you might want to consider taking more risks and moving out of your comfort zone more often.

Exploring My Understanding

Complete the following sentence: To me, *understanding my view of the world* means . . .

Considering My Options

Complete the following sentence: NOW I'm going to . . .

MAINTAINING MY PERSPECTIVE

We may see a situation a certain way and then learn that others think differently about it. There's a tendency to think we're not seeing it the right way and we acquiesce to the opinions of others. We give in because we feel our own ideas aren't substantial. We may feel that someone else knows better than we do. We give in because we don't trust our selves. We give in because it's a habit. We give in because it's difficult to stand up for our selves.

We are told "That's not the way it is" or "How can you see it that way?" or "You're not seeing what you think you're seeing." Such comments tend to corroborate our feelings and reasons for giving in. We begin to doubt our ability to see the world as we view it. We begin second guessing our judgment rather than exploring the opinions of others.

Certainly you want to benefit from others' experience and their points of view. You also want to maintain the integrity of your own experiences and feel confident with your feelings and views of reality. You have every right to experience your reality as you see it. Refrain from changing your perspective until you make a conscious choice to do so. Don't give in to the pressure from others' expectations to change your perspective until you have reason to make the change.

My Previous Experiences With Maintaining My Perspective

Write down your experiences with maintaining your perspective.

My Feelings About These Experiences

Write down your feelings about these experiences.

Suggested Exercise

Think about a situation in the past between you and another person, when you gave in or put aside your own point-of-view because you felt pressured to do so. Ask your self the following questions about that situation:

- How did you see the situation?
- How did the other person see it?
- For what reasons did you give in—change your opinion or judgment—to the other person's perspective?
- If you had to do it over again, would you?

- What can you do to avoid yielding to the pressure the next time a similar situation occurs?

Keep in mind that others have the right to maintain their perspectives even when it doesn't make sense to you!

Exploring My Understanding

Complete the following sentence: To me, *maintaining my perspective* means . . .

Considering My Options

Complete the following sentence: NOW I'm going to . . .

CHANGING MY PERSPECTIVE

There are times when it's appropriate to change your perspective about another person or situation. As we grow and develop, changes occur in our lives and in the way we look at the world, too. You may find that a preconceived notion about another person or situation is erroneous. You didn't have all of the facts about extenuating circumstances. Because of your perspective and the knowledge you had, you couldn't see the other person's point of view.

Your perspective changes over time because you change. Each of the lessons you've learned and the experiences you've had affect your view of the world. It's not unusual to find out that something you thought was fact is not true at all.

Changes also occur when you gain information from someone who holds a perspective that differs from yours. Given this new information, you can make a conscious choice to change your perspective. Making those conscious changes, rather than succumbing to subtle and perhaps not-so-subtle pressures, maintains your *gentle* control over life. Your choice to change must come from a conscious decision to revise what you believe to be true.

My Previous Experiences With Changing My Perspective

Write down your experiences with changing your perspective.

My Feelings About These Experiences

Write down your feelings about these experiences.

Suggested Exercise

Think about a person you know about whom your opinion has changed since you first met them.

- What was your original opinion?
- What is your opinion now?
- What transpired that changed your perspective about this person?
- How did you learn more about him or her?

- Did you make a conscious choice to change your perspective?
- Was there pressure from someone else to change your opinion about this person?

Keep in mind we are strongly influenced by first impressions and that we only get a glimpse of another person the first time we meet them.

Exploring My Understanding

Complete the following sentence: To me, *changing my perspective* means . . .

Considering My Options

Complete the following sentence: NOW I'm going to . . .

RESOLVING INTERNAL CONFLICTS

We often find our selves in situations and relationships where our minds are holding diametrically opposed, convoluted and confusing thoughts and feelings. The cognitive dissonance that is created makes us feel quite uncomfortable. Do you listen to your rational thoughts, the ideas from others or the messages from your heart?

Dissonance occurs when we hold one idea or belief to be true and also receive information to the contrary. No doubt you've experienced this phenomenon in a number of situations. Has your boss ever told you to do one thing and the policies of the company dictated another? Have you ever been in a discussion with a friend who expressed an opinion which drastically differed from the one espoused the day before?

When conflicting messages are received, your mind works diligently to resolve the conflict. Dealing with dissonance is uncomfortable and often difficult because it requires that you come to terms with differences within your self. You may choose to ignore the dissonance. You may choose to delay resolution of the conflict until you have more information, more incubation time or a readiness to resolve it. However you choose to act on the conflict needs to be a conscious choice. Experiencing cognitive dissonance is healthy because it's indicative of your own personal growth and development. It means you're getting to know your self better.

My Previous Experiences With Resolving Internal Conflicts

Write down your experiences with resolving internal conflicts.

My Feelings About These Experiences

Write down your feelings about these experiences.

Suggested Exercise

To resolve an internal conflict, use these steps:

1. On a sheet of paper, write down opposing or conflicting thoughts, ideas or feelings.
2. Identify the source of the conflict.
3. Decide if this is a conflict you want to resolve, ignore or postpone.
4. Determine the amount of time you want to contribute to addressing the dissonance.
5. Seek out additional information that you might need so you can understand the conflict more effectively.
6. Consider your responses to the questions:
    *   Am I holding onto the old information?
    *   Am I listening only to my emotions?
    *   Am I attending to only the rational explanation?
    *   What is the benefit for resolving the conflict?
    *   How will this resolution impact the rest of my life?
    *   Can I live without resolving this conflict?
    *   How will this resolution affect others?
    *   What's standing in my way of making a choice?
    *   What will I lose by resolving the conflict?
    *   What guidance am I receiving from my intuition?
7. Make a conscious choice about how you're going to deal with this internal conflict. Remember you can resolve it, ignore it or postpone your attention to it. Take action on your choice.

Exploring My Understanding

Complete the following sentence: To me, *resolving internal conflicts* means . . .

Considering My Options

Complete the following sentence: NOW I'm going to . . .

DEALING WITH CHALLENGES

When you find your self in a predicament, you say you have a problem. This problem conjures up a negative connotation because you know you'll have to expend time, energy and resources to find a solution. Problems definitely demand our attention. They often occur because we have a conflict with another, a situation didn't turn out the way we wanted it to, others didn't fulfill their end of the bargain, something breaks or an expectation is not met. As long as you think about problems as being negative, your desire to find resolutions may be weak. We generally don't like to deal with negativity of any kind.

One of the most effective ways of dealing with problems is to change your frame-of-reference. If you consider each of your problems as a challenge, your positive perspective will alter how you think about and deal with your predicaments.

Dealing with your challenges in a timely manner will eliminate the feeling of dread, make efficient use of your time, energy and resources and allow you to deal with other situations in your life. While it's true that some situations will take care of themselves, it's imperative that you make a conscious choice about each challenge in your life. Do you let it ride for a while? Do you deal with it immediately? Perhaps the most important question is: Is it a challenge? We frequently take on other people's challenges to avoid dealing with our own or to impose our desires on the outcome.

Each time we deal effectively with a challenge in our lives, the experience enhances our ability to deal with other challenges. It broadens our horizons. It augments our perspective. It gives us the opportunity to be responsible for our lives. With each challenge we acquire new information and learn lessons that are valuable to us as we pursue getting more of what we want in life.

My Previous Experiences With Dealing With Challenges

Write down your experiences with dealing with challenges.

My Feelings About These Experiences

Write down your feelings about these experiences.

Suggested Exercises

Once you've decided it's your responsibility to deal with a particular challenge, use the following techniques to gain a better understanding of the challenge and to find a resolution.

1. *Mindstorming*—Write your clearly stated challenge at the top of your page. Then take as much time as you need to list at least 25 ideas about how you can bring resolution to this challenge. Do not evaluate your ideas as you're writing them down (e.g., "This would never work" or "What a dumb idea!"). Your purpose is to generate as many ideas as possible. You'll find that the first five to ten ideas will come rather easily and that the last five will take longer to generate. Persevere. You may

have answers in those last ideas. Once you have your 25 ideas, combine those that could possibly work together. From your list you can select a few ideas that you might want to consider as possible solutions for your challenge. You can use this technique in combination with other techniques.

2. *Communing with Nature*—Take a walk in nature for a minimum of 30 minutes to let your mind explore possible solutions to challenges you're facing. It's best to be alone so you can hear the ideas that your mind generates. The more you release your cares and concerns of the day, the more room your mind will have to generate possibilities.

3. *Step-by-Step*—This technique is a rational approach to finding resolution for your challenges. If you use either of the other techniques mentioned, this approach will be even more effective for you.

    A. Clearly define the challenge in writing.
    B. List possible causes.
    C. Explore possible solutions. (Use *mindstorming* and *communing with nature*.)
    D. Identify the advantages and disadvantages of each possibility.
    E. Select the *most feasible* solution. (The optimal solution may be impossible or very difficult to put in place even though it would resolve the situation to your greatest satisfaction.)
    F. Make a plan for action to implement the solution.
    G. Implement your plan.
    H. Evaluate your conscious choice: Did this choice yield what I expected? Did I deal with this challenge effectively? What might I do differently next time?
    I. Move on to your next challenge!

Exploring My Understanding

Complete the following sentence: To me, *dealing with challenges* means . . .

Considering My Options

Complete the following sentence: NOW I'm going to . . .

MAXIMIZING MY BRAIN'S POWER

Results from recent research studies suggest that we have a virtually untapped reservoir for learning. The belief that our ability to learn new information and skills diminishes as we grow older is a myth. We have potential that will most likely not be realized during this lifetime. Tapping into your brain's power can be fun, stimulating and challenging. To use more of your brain power, you'll need to expend time, energy and resources. We use the power of the brain every time we learn something new, use our creative abilities, communicate, think, feel and act. The brain's power increases when we do things in a different way, think different thoughts, fully experience our emotions, expose our selves to different points-of-view and challenge our knowledge of how we go about thinking, feeling and doing.

There are certain abilities associated with the right and left sides of the brain. Those on the right side are aesthetic, emotional, symbolic, feeling and creative in nature. Those on the left side are rational, analytical, verbal and strategic. We use both sides of the brain when we transmit thoughts and experience feelings.

It's the emotional connection that aids in the storage of information in our memory banks. Depending on the situation and our point-of-view we will often favor one set of abilities over the other. For example, if a friend is sharing a challenge she is having with a boyfriend, you would tend to use your analytical and verbal skills. If you are having a similar challenge with your friend, your emotive responses would be more prominent. Most things depend on how you view them.

Maintaining a balance among the dimensions of your life will enhance your ability to more fully use the power of your brain. When you take care of your self physically, you enjoy a sharper clarity of thought. If you neglect your self emotionally, your emotionality will interfere with rational thought. The more you maximize the use of your brain, the more you'll be able to create the world that you want to live in.

My Previous Experiences With Maximizing My Brain's Power

Write down your experiences with maximizing your brain's power.

My Feelings About These Experiences

Write down your feelings about these experiences.

Suggested Exercise

To stretch your mental capacity and stimulate the power of your brain, look for opportunities to learn new information and expand your experiences. Here are some suggested activities:

- Engage in brain teasers.
- Expand your vocabulary.
- Work puzzles.
- Learn a new language.
- Take up a new hobby.
- Get to know people whose cultural background differs significantly from your own.
- Take a course in enhancing your memory.
- Substitute pictures for words.
- Learn a craft.

Learning how to do anything that you don't already know will help. While you're engaged in the learning process, create an environment that allows enjoyment of the activities. Include playing baroque or neo-classical music in the background. This type of music relaxes the brain, increases knowledge retention and enhances the learning process. The brain tends to be more susceptible when the music engages the right side of the brain while feeding information to the left side of the brain. We all learn more when we're having fun and are relaxed.

Exploring My Understanding

Complete the following sentence: To me, *maximizing my brain's power* means . . .

Considering My Options

Complete the following sentence: NOW I'm going to . . .

ENHANCING MY CREATIVITY

Are you curious, wondering how things work? Are you willing to take risks and try something new? Do you like change because it's stimulating? Do you challenge the status quo? Do you sometimes just know a particular solution will be a great one? Whether you've answered "yes" or "no," you have the capacity for being creative.

We often think that being creative means that we have to possess the great talents of an artist, dancer, singer, designer or architect. In actuality, creativity is simply looking at the situation using a novel or unusual point of view. We all have creative abilities—we just don't use them.

We can learn much about being creative from children. By nature, children are very curious and quite unique in their approach to the world. Until adults tell them (which over time tends to squelch their creative explorations), children don't know how things are suppose to be. Creativity is squelched by comments such as, "That's not how you do it!" "We tried doing it that way before and it was a disaster," and "Don't rock the boat."

By being creative, we make our world a much more interesting and stimulating place to live. Creativity is an essential element in maximizing your time, energy and resources. A synergy between both sides of your brain emerges from the stimulation created by new and unusual ideas. You're more likely to take risks and move out of your comfort zone. Your decisions are more effective and resolutions to challenges are more satisfying. You add spark and enthusiasm to your relationships. You learn more. Keep in mind there is always more than one right way to do everything!

My Previous Experiences With Enhancing My Creativity

Write down your experiences with enhancing your creativity.

My Feelings About These Experiences

Write down your feelings about these experiences.

Suggested Exercise

1. Select a common object, such as a paper clip, a rubber band, a cup or a shoe. Think about the many ways you can use it in addition to its commonly accepted use. For example, a paper clip could be an earring, a tool for picking locks or a weapon. See how many different uses you can identify. This exercise is fun to do with friends, too.

2. What can you create out of what's in the box on the following page? (Your response will be correct, no matter what it is.)

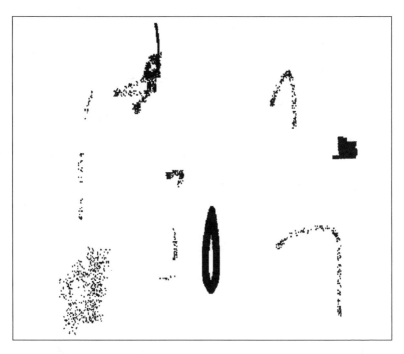

Exploring My Understanding

Complete the following sentence: To me, *enhancing my creativity* means . . .

Considering My Options

Complete the following sentence: NOW I'm going to . . .

TAKING RISKS

We're not risk-takers, but we like to think we are. We fear failure and looking ridiculous. We seek the sure thing. We want to know what's on the other side of a decision before we'll commit to it.

Taking calculated risks is not seeking thrills or putting your self in physical or psychological danger. Taking calculated risks means you're willing to extend your experience beyond what you've encountered up to this point in life. It's meeting life's challenges without giving up. It's going after what you want when others attempt to deter you. It's trusting your intuition when all of the facts are not clear. It's planning for action—being proactive rather than reactive. It's moving out of your comfort zone so you can learn more about your self and your world. Some examples of risk-taking might include opening your own business, asking someone to marry you, having a child, moving to a new location, changing jobs, dissolving a relationship, sampling a new food or doing the opposite of what's expected.

What defines a risk-taking behavior is an individual matter. The elements inherent in calculated risk-taking include having an experience for the first time, moving from a known situation into an unknown and feeling some anxiety about engaging in the new behavior. You must be willing to fail, feel ridiculous and accept the scorn of others who'll say, "I told you so!" You must be willing to learn something new about your self and be willing to face whatever consequences result from your actions.

The more risks you take, the more confident you'll become in your ability to bounce back if the situation doesn't work out for your benefit or meet your desired level of satisfaction. Taking risks gives you more options; You sample more of what life has to offer. You'll find your enjoyment is enhanced by the increased knowledge you have about your self.

My Previous Experiences With Taking Risks

Write down your experiences with taking risks.

My Feelings About These Experiences

Write down your feelings about these experiences.

Suggested Exercise

Make an agreement with your self to engage in a calculated risk-taking behavior at least once a month. Keep in mind that what's risky to you may not be risky for another person. Identify and list the risk-taking behaviors that you want to experience. Select activities that will move you out of your comfort zone and into a broader perspective about life and your experience with it. To get your brain juices flowing, here are some suggestions that may be "risky" for you:

- Rearrange the furniture.
- Go out to eat in an expensive restaurant alone.
- Take flying or scuba lessons.
- Ski in the Alps.
- Work on a house-building community project.
- Tell someone what you think or how you feel about them.
- Change your hairstyle.
- Meet your neighbors.
- Travel abroad.
- Dance the *lambada*.

The list is endless. Have fun!

Exploring My Understanding

Complete the following sentence: To me, *taking risks* means . . .

Considering My Options

Complete the following sentence: NOW, I'm going to . . .

MAKING EFFECTIVE DECISIONS

We frequently decide not to decide when it comes to making decisions. We're not sure if the decision we make is going to be the right one. We don't have confidence in our ability to use the knowledge we have. We feel we don't have enough information to decide. We're concerned about what others might do or what they might want us to do. Refusing to emphatically decide about situations in our lives tends to leave our destinies to chance.

When we are effective decision makers, we are taking responsibility for our lives and the outcomes of those decisions. We're concerned about making the best decision so we want to exhaust all of our options, weigh the advantages and disadvantages, mull the situation over and play out each scenario.

It's virtually impossible and totally unrealistic to exhaust every option. The options are innumerable. So the best decision is the one you make given the information you have at the time you need to make your decision.

It's beneficial to target the most effective decision—the one that will be possible for you and your situation. You must consider what investment of your time, energy and resources will be required.

Not every decision is a life-significant or life-threatening one. Keep your perspective about the importance of each decision. If you make a decision that doesn't work out the way you anticipated it would, you always have the option of making another one. Just because a decision is ineffective in addressing the situation doesn't mean you're a failure, or you can't make effective decisions or that the world is going to come to an end!

Making decisions is being responsible for your life. In order to get what you want, you must make decisions that will have a beneficial impact on you. Although your decisions will impact others, take whatever action is best for you.

My Previous Experiences With Making Effective Decisions

Write down your experiences with making effective decisions.

My Feelings About These Experiences

Write down your feelings about these experiences.

Suggested Exercise

When you have a decision to make, consider using these questions to gather the kind of information you need:

1. Is this a decision that is mine to make? Am I responsible for the outcome of the situation? If your answer is "no," be willing to let the people responsible take care of the situation.
2. What is my time frame? Choose a specific date by which you need to decide. Give your self enough time to think about the situation. Refrain from using *whenever* as your time frame.
3. What are my options? Look at the situation from different points-of-view. Identify the advantages and disadvantages of each option. Consider how each option will positively and negatively impact you.
4. How will the choices I make impact others? Consider how the consequences of your actions benefit others as well as infringe upon their rights.
5. Is my choice consistent with my value system? Refrain from making choices that conflict with what you hold to be true and important.
6. Can I feasibly implement this decision? No matter how terrific the decision is, if you can't implement it, it won't work.
7. What does my intuition tell me to do? Ask your self, "Is this the best decision for me to make at this point in time?" Listen for the response. Your "gut" will support your direction and your purpose if you listen and respond accordingly.

Exploring My Understanding

Complete the following sentence: To me, *making effective decisions* means . . .

Considering My Options

Complete the following sentence: NOW I'm going to . . .

LEARNING THROUGH MY EXPERIENCES

Every experience you have is a gift and an opportunity for learning more about your self, others and the world. Every lesson of life gives you a mechanism for maximizing your potential, for expanding your knowledge base and for fully experiencing who you are.

Many of our lessons are easy; we only have to hear the "teacher" once and we understand the facts and what needs to be done. Or we only need one demonstration and we can figure out how to tie a shoe or water the plants. The most important lessons in life seem to be the ones that are initially unpleasant, painful and require a great deal of energy on our parts.

Each lesson we encounter serves a purpose. Each lesson helps us move closer to what we want in life. Each lesson provides direction if we pay attention.

If you ever wonder why you keep having the same experiences over and over again, consider if you've heard the message in that experience. Make every effort to capitalize on what transpires in your life. Your efforts will lead to a richer and more rewarding reality.

My Previous Experiences With Learning Through My Experiences

Write down your thoughts about learning through your experiences.

My Feelings About These Experiences

Write down your feelings about these experiences.

Suggested Exercise

Think about something you now do as a result of an experience you've had in your life. How quickly did you learn the lesson? Did you require many trials? Do you use that information on a regular basis? How has this knowledge impacted your life? As you move through life, look for those lessons that enhance your living.

Exploring My Understanding

Complete the following sentence: To me, *learning through my experiences* means . . .

Considering My Options

Complete the following sentence: NOW I'm going to . . .

7
Growing InSync with the Physical Dimension

Our bodies are conduits through which we experience life. The manner in which we care for our bodies has a direct effect on the other dimensions in our lives. When we maintain a healthy body, our ability to make decisions, be more creative and think clearly are enhanced. Our relationships are more dynamic and fluid, allowing us to concentrate on maximizing the connection with others rather than complaining about what ails us. A healthy body contributes to the health of our emotions. When our bodies are well-maintained, we have more energy to deal with the aspects of our emotional dimension. A well-maintained body also allows us freedom to pursue our visions in life and to clearly articulate our purposes.

Too often the focus in the physical dimension is on how the body looks. The media, other people and past experiences push us to be concerned about our looks. We're bombarded with information that reminds us we don't have perfect bodies. Many "remedies" (perfumes, cars, diets, exercises, exercise equipment) promise that our body will be sought after for its beauty. That perpetuated fantasy can create undue anxiety for those of us who would never be featured on the cover of a magazine.

This superficial approach to taking care of our bodies is just that—superficial. Having a calendar pin-up's body makes no lasting contribution to the persons we really are. Taking care of and nurturing our bodies contributes significantly to being the person we want to be. Our bodies act as the vehicle for carrying out our responsibilities and for getting what we want out of life. If we maintain physical fitness in every sense of the phrase, then we have the energy to do all that we want to do with our lives.

It's quite likely you already know a lot about your physical dimension. Information about how to exercise and eat right is easily accessible. By engaging in the exercises in this chapter, such as those about exercising aerobically, increasing your flexibility and limiting cholesterol, sugars and caffeine, you'll learn ways to put things into action that you probably already know but don't use.

A Special Note:

Keep in mind that the directions encourage you to listen to your body. This information is general in nature and is not a substitute for professional advice from doctors, physiologists, nutritionists and other health-related professionals. If you have a serious problem or one that is causing you concern, take responsible action on your own behalf. Find the professional who can help you meet your needs.

Please refer to page 40 for directions on how to maximize your experiences.

LOVING MY BODY

Given the opportunity, most of us would change something about our bodies. Some of us feel we have too much fat and too little muscle. Others don't like their thighs, their nose or their skin. Still others aren't happy with the way their bodies function—upset stomachs, headaches and slow digestive systems. We typically say things like, "I hate my nose" or "I'm sick and tired of these headaches."

There are some things about our bodies that we are given through the genes of our parents, such as our height. We have no control over them nor can we change them. Yet, there are a number of things we can change. First, we must accept and love our bodies for being the incredible organisms they are. Accepting and loving our bodies change them. By making friends with our bodies rather than viewing them as our enemies, we can feel comfortable with how our bodies look and feel.

My Previous Experiences With Loving My Body

Write down your experiences with loving your body.

My Feelings About These Experiences

Write down your feelings about these experiences.

Suggested Exercise

This simple exercise is one way to begin the process of accepting and loving your body. Begin by saying to your self out loud, "I love my toes. I love my feet. I love my ankles." Move all around your body, including limbs, torso and head.

Go inside your body and express love and acceptance for your organs—lungs, heart and liver—and your body's functions—digestion, breathing and circulation. Make a concerted effort to include those parts of your body you're not happy with or would like to change. Repeat these statements with enthusiasm, even if you don't feel enthusiastic at first. Use this exercise at least once a day. You can do it while you're relaxing, exercising or driving.

Exploring My Understanding

Complete the following sentence: To me, *loving my body* means . . .

Considering My Options

Complete the following sentence: NOW I'm going to . . .

EXPERIENCING MY SENSES

We tend to take our senses for granted. The only time we really pay attention to them is when they're not working properly. We think about our eyes when we can't see too well without corrective lenses. We think about our ears when we can't hear too well without assistance or when we have an earache. We think about our noses and our sense of smell when we have a cold or sinus trouble and can't smell. We think about our taste buds when they are dulled by the same cold or sinus condition. We think about our sense of touch when our skin is sunburned and we feel the pain when touched. We short-change our experience in life if we only think of our senses when they're out of commission.

Our senses convey information about our environment and experiences to our being. About 80 percent of what we know about our world comes through our sense of sight. Our sense of smell is perhaps the most powerful of all senses in bringing back memories that are deeply embedded.

When was the last time you stared intently at a sight that was overwhelming, either too beautiful or too horrible to look at? Did you see all of the colors that made the sight memorable? Did you listen to the sounds—the birds, the wind, the cars passing by, the cries and the moans? Did you smell the aromas—the fragrance of perfume, the bouquet of flowers, the odor of a sewer, the scent from a bakery? Were your taste buds stimulated by the smells and the sights? Did you feel the wind in your hair, the sun on you neck, the dampness in your bones? When we "listen" to our senses, our awareness of our world is heightened. We gain new knowledge and insight into our selves, others and the world in which we live.

My Previous Experiences With Experiencing My Senses

Write down your experiences with your senses.

My Feelings About These Experiences

Write down your feelings about these experiences.

Suggested Exercises

1. To experience your **sense of sight**, designate a day to really look at the world around you. Your purpose is to *observe* not to judge what you see. Begin by taking a very good look at your self in the morning's mirror. Look at your face, your eyes, your nose and your skin. Look at the people who share the breakfast table with you. Notice their eyes, their smiles, their clothes, their gait. Look at the inside of your car, the car in front of you, the trees along the road as you're stopped in traffic. Take a good look at the attendant in the parking garage, the people on the elevator and your co-workers. These ideas are just starters. Look at your world with purpose and intent. Look at what you've been missing.

2. To experience your **sense of hearing**, designate a day to really listen to the sounds around you. Listen to the birds singing in the early morning. Listen to the chatter of your children. Listen as you start your car or hear the brakes screech from the bus or train as it pulls up to your stop. Listen to the sounds made by your computer as you turn it on. Listen to the ticking of a clock. These ideas are just starters. Listen to your world with purpose and intent. Listen to what you've been missing.

3. To experience your **sense of smell**, designate a day to really smell the aromas in your environment. Smell your after-shave lotion or your perfume. Smell the bar of soap you use to wash your body. Smell the odor from your jogging shoes. Smell the stench in the garbage can. Smell the freshly cut wood. These ideas are just starters. Smell your world with purpose and intent. Smell the aromas and odors you've been missing.

4. To experience your **sense of taste**, designate a day to really taste the food you put in your mouth. Identify the tastes as sweet, bitter, sour, salty, astringent and pungent. How does the banana taste? What about the

lemon in your tea? What sensation do you get when you taste yogurt? When you taste your food on this day, take small bites. Chew each bite slowly, stimulating your taste buds. Savor the tastes. What do you like about the taste? What don't you like? Taste your world with purpose and intent. Taste your food to experience those tastes you've been missing.

5. To experience your **sense of touch**, designate a day to really touch the things in your environment. Identify those objects that are smooth, hard, rough, soft, slick, bumpy and textured to the touch. How do the sheets feel on your skin? What does the washcloth feel like on your face? How does the brush feel on your gums? What do the petals of a daisy feel like? Does your steering wheel feel smooth? How about walking in dirt or sand, what does that feel like? These ideas are just starters. Touch your world with purpose and intent. Experience the sense of touch you've been missing.

Exploring My Understanding

Complete the following sentence: To me, *experiencing my senses* means . . .

Considering My Options

Complete the following sentence: NOW I'm going to . . .

RESTING MY BODY

How much rest and sleep does your body need? Many experts tell us everyone needs at least eight hours of sleep in order for our bodies and minds to function optimally. Yet, because of our individual differences and genetic make-ups, our sleep needs can be as individualistic as our voices. Resting your body is essential because the body needs time to repair the damage it encounters throughout the awake state. As a result of adequate rest and sleep, you'll become energized and eager to face the new day. Keep in mind your body needs more time for resting and sleeping when you're feeling excessive stress.

My Previous Experiences With Resting My Body

Write down your experiences with resting your body.

My Feelings About These Experiences

Write down your feelings about these experiences.

Suggested Exercise

To find out how much rest and sleep your body really needs, use this exercise: For a week or possibly two, go to bed at a certain time each evening, such as 10:00, and wake up without an alarm clock. Make a note of the time you wake up each morning. Take the average of the times you woke up at the end of your experiment. Then you'll know how much sleep you need each evening.

Exploring My Understanding

Complete the following sentence: To me, *resting my body* means . . .

Considering My Options

Complete the following sentence: NOW I'm going to . . .

SCANNING MY BODY

Throughout the day, your body absorbs the many stressors that you encounter. Many of the stressors—someone pulling out in front of you on the interstate, your boss speaking to you tersely, a shipment arriving late, the dog running away—may seem insignificant, inconsequential and part of the daily routine.

Your body responds physiologically to every stress you experience. This physiological response is stored in your body, often in the form of lactic acid. The cumulative effect makes your muscles tense and tired. You often don't even notice until you get into a crisis. Then your neck becomes tense and you have a headache that won't go away. If you take the time to scan your body, to notice the tense areas, you can reduce the tenseness and fatigue.

My Previous Experiences With Scanning My Body

Write down your experiences with scanning your body.

My Feelings About These Experiences

Write down your feelings about these experiences.

Suggested Exercises

1. Several times throughout the day, take a few moments to scan your body for tense and tight muscles. Begin in one area, moving to other areas to check out all muscle groups. When you find a tense area, gently stretch or massage it. Then go on to the next area. Focus on your stress points—neck, shoulders and chest. Most of us have particular areas that tend to be tenser than others.

2. Pay attention to your hands. Make a very tight fist and hold it for approximately 15 seconds, then release your hand. The tensing and releasing is another way to relieve the stress.

Be in tune with your body through awareness. You can do these exercises just about anywhere and at any time: sitting in traffic, sitting at your desk, taking a break, watching television or enjoying quiet time.

Exploring My Understanding

Complete the following sentence: To me, *scanning my body* means . . .

Considering My Options

Complete the following sentence: NOW I'm going to . . .

RELAXING MY BODY

Our bodies need time to relax every day because of the stressors we encounter. We also need time for relaxation to regain mental clarity, quiet our minds from endless thought-racing and enjoy just being with our selves.

We often think about what we can do to relax. Let's consider relaxation from a different point of view and think about how we can just "be" for a few minutes. Think about the last time you relaxed your body. What did you do? Did you read a book, watch TV or take a walk? When was the last time you sat or reclined quietly, doing nothing except breathing?

My Previous Experiences With Relaxing My Body

Write down your experiences with relaxing your body.

My Feelings About These Experiences

Write down your feelings about these experiences.

Suggested Exercises

There are many ways to relax your body by just "being," including progressive relaxation, massage and yoga. Here are a couple of simple techniques for you to sample:

1. Sit or recline comfortably in a quiet place where you'll not be disturbed. Close your eyes. Clear your mind of all thoughts. Begin breathing deeply and evenly by filling up your lungs and entire abdominal cavity with air. Release your breath slowly through the nose to a count of five. As you breathe out, release the tension and worries that you've accumulated during the day. Continue to breathe in and out for at least five minutes. You can extend the time as you become comfortable with the exercise. Sweep away any thoughts that come into your mind. Know that they'll return once you resume your normal activity. You can repeat this exercise at anytime. A good time to use it is when you're feeling out of balance or frustrated.
2. Sit or recline comfortably in a quiet place where you'll not be disturbed. Close your eyes. Clear your mind of any thoughts. Picture the number "1" in your mind and focus on it. Begin breathing deeply and evenly, filling up your lungs and your entire abdominal cavity with air. As you breathe out, say "one" either to your self or audibly. Keep your focus on the number "1" in your mind. Remember to say "one" each time you breathe out. Continue this exercise for at least five minutes. It's

recommended that you spend 20 minutes with this exercise. Again, extend the time as you become comfortable with it. (This exercise is an adaptation of Herbert Benson's Relaxation Response.)

Exploring My Understanding

Complete the following sentence: To me, *relaxing my body* means . . .

Considering My Options

Complete the following sentence: NOW I'm going to . . .

VALUING MY SEXUALITY

Too often we're expected to ignore or deny our sexuality. Religious and social taboos inhibit us from thinking about and expressing how we feel about our gender. Our gender is a fundamental part of who we are. We are sexual beings, male or female.

We recognize our uniqueness as a human being when we accept, value and respect our sexuality. By respecting our sexuality, we demonstrate respect for our selves and others.

Gender not only affects us physically, it also affects our view of the world and how we respond to it. Gender affects our communication. Gender affects our relationships.

Be cognizant that your body is your own. You can choose

how you feel. You can choose how you enjoy your body. You can express and enjoy your sexuality alone or with another. Keep in mind that physically encountering another is just one way to express your sexual nature.

My Previous Experiences With Valuing My Sexuality

Write down your experiences with valuing your sexuality.

My Feelings About These Experiences

Write down your feelings about these experiences.

Suggested Exercises

1. Spend some time alone with your self. Think about how you really feel and what you really think about your maleness or femaleness. (If the tapes inside your head tell you that "sex is off-limits," push past that thought. You can think whatever it is you want to think.) Think about the body parts that are a manifestation of your gender. Think about how you view the world.

2. Spend some time looking at your body without clothes. What do you see? What makes you uniquely female or male?

3. Look for ways to express and enjoy your sexuality alone and with others. Do you enjoy writing poems?

Are you a dancer? Do you write music? Can you paint how you feel? How does your body feel? What pleasure do you feel from touch?

4. Make conscious choices about sharing your body with another. Refrain from responding to coercion or expectations. Remember: it's your body. You're the only one who has the right to make choices about it. In turn, when you want others to share their bodies with you, respect their choices. They may not want to share with you at that time.

5. Spend some time with a friend of the opposite gender. Talk about the differences in how you view the world, how you communicate and how you express your gender. You'll feel a sense of appreciation for your own gender as well as that of your friend.

Exploring My Understanding

Complete the following sentence: To me, *valuing my sexuality* means . . .

Considering My Options

Complete the following sentence: NOW I'm going to . . .

EXERCISING MY BODY REGULARLY

Although we're no longer running from wild animals for survival, our bodies are made for moving. Today we must make an effort to exercise regularly to counteract our sedentary lifestyle.

We all know the merits of exercising our bodies. Exercise reduces stress, helps bodily functions work properly, stimulates growth and enhances mental clarity. The excuses we offer for not exercising are many and varied: "I don't have enough time," "I don't have a good place to exercise" or "I'm just too tired."

If you want to get the most out of your life, it's important for exercise to become a habit—an integral part of your routine. You can select a variety of exercises that are available to you. Tennis, bowling, walking, hiking, rollerblading and canoeing are all enjoyable activities. When exercise is a priority in your life, you'll have more energy for all the other things you want to do.

My Previous Experiences With Exercising My Body Regularly

Write down your experiences with exercising your body regularly.

My Feelings About These Experiences

Write down your feelings about these experiences.

Suggested Exercise

To make exercise part of your regular routine, consider these suggestions:

1. Select exercises you enjoy. It's important to have a number of exercises you can be involved with so you don't get bored with doing the same thing over and over again.

2. Decide where you'll exercise. Do you prefer a controlled environment like a health club? Do you have a great neighborhood for walking? Do you have tennis courts close to your work? The place must be convenient for you during the time you want to exercise.

3. Find several partners. If you prefer to exercise with others, having several partners is a good idea. When you only have one exercise partner, your routine can be disrupted when your partner is sick, out-of-town or unmotivated.

4. Schedule your exercise time when you will not be interrupted or distracted. For example, some prefer to exercise first thing in the morning before the busy day starts. Others like to exercise after work and before dinner, while others like to exercise at lunch time. Find what works for you.

5. Set up a schedule for exercise. At the beginning of your week, decide which days you're going to exercise and put that time on your calendar. You may choose to play tennis twice a week and walk on the local high school track three mornings for your aerobic workout. Do something daily to move your body.

6. Stretch before and after any exercise. Stretching before exercising elongates the muscles so they will be more flexible. This flexibility decreases the likelihood of injury. Stretching the muscles used during the exercise afterwards, releases the tension and decreases the buildup of lactic acid.

7. Chart your progress to keep your self in the routine. When you have reached and maintained your goal of exercising your body regularly, commend your self in any way you choose. Choose something tangible or intangible that's important to you. EXCEPTION: Avoid using food as your reward.

Exploring My Understanding

Complete the following sentence: To me, *exercising my body regularly* means . . .

Considering My Options

Complete the following sentence: NOW I'm going to . . .

EXERCISING MY BODY AEROBICALLY

Aerobic exercise is important for stimulating the heart muscle, increasing circulation and expanding the capacity of the lungs. A game of touch football on a Saturday afternoon or a leisurely walk around a lake is not aerobic.

You are exercising aerobically when your heart rate is in its target heart rate (THR) zone. (See charts for the formulas to determine your target heart rate zone.) To determine if you're working within your THR zone, take your pulse at your wrist for 10 seconds and multiply that number by six. Compare that number to your THR range. It's recommended that you exercise aerobically for 20 to 30 minutes continuously, three times a week.

Aerobic exercises include swimming, cross country skiing, race walking, biking, jogging, rowing, Step/bench classes, aerobics classes, dancing and climbing stairs. Although tennis and golf (if you walk) are great exercises, they are not by nature aerobic because there is a lot of stopping and starting. Think about how you exercise aerobically.

Determine Your Target Heart Rate (THR) Zone

FOR MEN

205 – _____ = _____
       1/2 your age   maximum heart rate

_____ X .60 = _____
maximum heart rate   low end of zone

_____ X .80 = _____
maximum heart rate   high end of zone

FOR WOMEN

205 – _____ = _____
        your age   maximum heart rate

_____ X .60 = _____
maximum heart rate   low end of zone

_____ X .80 = _____
maximum heart rate   high end of zone

To get the most benefit out of your aerobic workout, your pulse rate needs to be within the low and high ends of your THR.

My Previous Experiences With Exercising My Body Aerobically:

Write down your experiences with exercising aerobically.

My Feelings About These Experiences

Write down your feelings about these experiences.

Suggested Exercises:

1. Select two or three aerobic exercises you enjoy. Cross-training is a more effective way of exercising your body. It prevents injury because you're not overusing the same muscle groups continuously. A variety of exercises also decreases boredom.
2. Read "Exercising My Body" for other suggestions about making exercise part of your regular routine.

Exploring My Understanding:

Complete the following sentence: To me, *exercising my body aerobically* means . . .

Considering My Options:

Complete the following sentence: NOW I'm going to . . .

INCREASING MY FLEXIBILITY

Flexibility is the ability of each body joint to bend, stretch and twist through the full range of motion. The best way to increase our flexibility is through stretching. Stretching elongates the muscles, tendons and ligaments.

The benefits of being flexible include enhancing athletic performance, reducing risk of becoming injured, reducing stress and tension, warming up and cooling down the muscles and being in tune with your body. Stretching also keeps you mentally sharp.

My Previous Experiences With Increasing My Flexibility

Write down your experiences with increasing your flexibility.

My Feelings About These Experiences

Write down your feelings about these experiences.

Suggested Exercises

1. Stretch before and after any exercise. Pay particular attention to those muscle groups that are most involved in the exercise.
2. Take yoga lessons. Hatha yoga is an excellent way to stretch your muscles and relax your body. Classes are available through most community continuing education programs at colleges and universities. Centers, clinics and instructors offer group as well as individual classes. Ask around for recommendations. You may want to try several instructors.
3. Take stretch breaks. Anytime your body's feeling tense, take the time to stretch your muscles. Stretching first thing in the morning awakens your muscles and readies your body for the day. Stretching last thing in the evening releases tension and toxins that have built up in your body from the day's stress. You can also stretch while sitting at your desk, watching a movie or taking a break. The stretching will refresh you, release pent up energy and increase your flexibility. If you work at a desk most of the day, consider taking a stretch break every 15 minutes.

Exploring My Understanding

Complete the following sentence: To me, *increasing my flexibility* means . . .

Considering My Options:

Complete the following sentence: NOW I'm going to . . .

INCREASING MY STRENGTH

Strength is the ability of the muscles to resist force, including the force of gravity. When we think about strength, we often have a picture of Mr. Atlas with bulging muscles lifting massive amounts of weight over his head. This type of strength is for the extraordinary and is unrealistic for the majority of us.

When you think about increasing your strength, keep in mind that your muscles allow you to move freely. You need strength for lifting, turning, pulling and pushing activities that you come across in your daily life. Turning the steering wheel of a vehicle that doesn't have power steering, opening a jar and lifting a box all require strength. Maintaining strong muscles also maximizes the use of your bones and decreases the amount of fat in your body.

My Previous Experiences With Increasing My Strength

Write down your experiences with increasing your strength.

My Feelings About These Experiences

Write down your feelings about these experiences.

Suggested Exercises

1. If you are a novice at strength training, work with a personal trainer to set up a program and routine. There are

a number of good books written by body builders for both men and women that can also serve as resource guides. The advantage of using a trainer is to learn proper technique and form, which is critical for maximizing your efforts and avoiding injury. Keep in mind your routine doesn't have to be elaborate or intensive. Develop a routine with your trainer that works for you. Your routine may vary greatly from what another person might do. This is not a time to compare what you're doing or how much weight you're pressing or not pressing! Keep in mind that your purpose is to strengthen your muscles.

2. Use appropriate equipment. Many people weight train at a health club or gym because of the variety of weights that are available. You can set up a gym in your home. If you decide to do so, be sure you use expert advice when you select your equipment. Universal machines and free weights can be convenient but expensive to have at home.

    There are many types of equipment that can be used, including Keiser, Nautilus, David and Cybex (all machines) in addition to free weights. Clubs and gyms often have at least one set of machines. Larger clubs often have a wider selection of machines to use. Use whatever equipment works best for you.

3. Workout with a partner. A partner can spot you when you're lifting, give you a break between sets and be a good source of motivation. Working out with a partner is not required because you'll find that there is always someone who is more than willing to spot you when you need it. People who work out in clubs or gyms often develop a camaraderie.

4. Schedule your workout time. In order to receive benefit from your strength training it needs to be regular. Each muscle group of your body needs a workout at least twice a week in order to maintain the muscle mass

you're developing. You'll want to take at least a 48-hour rest between workouts for each muscle group because you tear your muscles each time you add weight to your movements. The 48-hour time period gives your muscles time to repair. You may want to combine your strength training activity with your aerobic workout. Experiment to determine if doing your aerobic activity prior to your weight training is preferable to doing it afterwards.

5. Stretch before and after your training. Stretching your muscles (increasing your flexibility) reduces the risk of injury. After your initial warm-up, consider adding a ten-minute aerobic activity, such as biking or walking on a treadmill, prior to your weight workout. Warm muscles are less prone to injury than are cold muscles. After your workout, be sure to stretch. Stretching will elongate the muscles, release the tension and decrease the buildup of lactic acid.

6. Chart your progress to keep your self in a routine. As you work towards increasing your strength, commend your self. The way you commend your self is up to you. Choose something tangible or intangible that's important to you. EXCEPTION: Avoid using food as your reward.

Exploring My Understanding

Complete the following sentence: To me, *increasing my strength* means . . .

Considering My Options

Complete the following sentence: NOW I'm going to . . .

INCREASING MY ENDURANCE

Endurance is the ability to physically move for a period of time without tiring. Endurance is one indication of how physically fit you are. It uses both aerobic capacity and muscle strength. Think about how you fare on a long walk in a hilly or mountainous area. Do your muscles and lungs serve you well or are you out of breath on the ascent? Do your muscles ache because they are flaccid and weak?

Increasing your endurance is easy when you're involved in both aerobic and strength training activities. The benefits include improved functioning of the lungs and circulatory system, increased ability to transport oxygen to all parts of the body, increased efficiency of the heart muscle, enhanced mental clarity and the ability to survive potentially dangerous situations in elements of nature (i.e., your boat overturns, you get lost on a hike).

My Previous Experiences With Increasing My Endurance

Write down your experiences with increasing your endurance.

My Feelings About These Experiences

Write down your feelings about these experiences.

Suggested Exercises

1. *The Sit-Up Test.* One way to measure your level of endurance is to do as many sit-ups as you're able within a 60-second time period. Doing bent-knee sit ups, count how many you do. It usually helps if you have someone hold your feet and count for you. Record that number. You can do this test as often as you'd like to chart your progress.

2. *The "I-Ache Now" Exercise.* Keep a record of how far you get into an activity before you're feeling out-of-breath and/or a strain on your muscles. Include in your record the date, type of activity, location of activity and the number of minutes you felt comfortable in the activity. If you've added aerobic and strength training exercises to your routine, you'll be able to see the progress you're making over time.

3. *The Extended Endurance Test.* About every six months, test your endurance by engaging in one aerobic activity continuously until exhaustion. Activities that are particularly conducive to this endurance test include swimming, biking, jogging or step climbing. Record your time and compare it to your next test of extended endurance.

Exploring My Understanding

Complete the following sentence: To me, *increasing my endurance* means . . .

Considering My Options

Complete the following sentence: NOW I'm going to . . .

INCREASING MY LEAN MUSCLE MASS

Physical fitness experts are now telling us that one of the most accurate measures of our physical fitness is the ratio of lean muscle mass to the fat in our bodies. Knowing how much you weigh is not a good indicator of how much lean muscle mass you carry. Weight charts can be misleading because they are not adaptable to individual needs nor do they take into consideration the genetic make-up of the body.

Body fat is necessary for a healthy body. We need some fat to cushion the organs and generate energy, but too much fat is dangerous to our health. The average percent of body fat recommended for adult males under 40, is 18 percent and for adult females is no more than 24 percent. For males over 40, the recommended body fat percentage is 18 percent and 28 percent for females in the same age category. The amount of body fat tends to vary with age. When you increase your muscle mass through aerobic activity and weight training, you decrease your body's fat content. Aerobic activity is the most effective way of burning off your fat. Every effort needs to be made to maintain an appropriate proportion of lean muscle mass to fat in the body.

My Previous Experiences With Increasing My Lean Muscle Mass

Write down your experiences with increasing your lean muscle mass.

My Feelings About These Experiences

Write down your feelings about these experiences.

Suggested Exercises

To determine your current lean muscle mass to fat ratio, here are a couple of suggestions:

1. *The Skin-Fold Test.* An exercise physiologist can measure the body's fat content by using calipers that measure the number of skin-folds at three points on your body. For men, the count is taken on the chest, in the abdominal area and on the thigh. For women, the count is taken under the arm, in the pelvic area and on the thigh. The three counts are added together for a total which is used to find the body fat content on a chart according to your age.

2. *The Do-It-Your Self Test.* This test is an unscientific, yet revealing self-assessment. Remove all of your clothes

and stand in front of a full length mirror. Look at your body and determine how you feel about your image in the mirror. Gently pinch different areas of your body. If you can pinch more than an inch, your body may be carrying around more fat than is necessary.

3. To increase your lean muscle mass, consider reviewing the following exercises: "Limiting Fats," "Limiting Cholesterol," "Eating a Variety of Foods," "Drinking Water," "Exercising My Body Aerobically," and "Increasing My Strength."

Exploring My Understanding

Complete the following sentence: To me, *increasing my lean muscle mass* means . . .

Considering My Options

Complete the following exercises: NOW I'm going to . . .

EATING REGULARLY

Our bodies are remarkable quantum mechanical machines that require fuel on a regular basis. The body requires fueling after a night's sleep and about every four waking hours. Four hours is approximately how long it takes for the body to process the meal you eat.

We need to listen to our bodies and eat only when we're

hungry. We'll be hungry on a regular basis if we eat smaller rather than larger meals and stop eating before we are too full. Skipping meals and overeating puts stress on the body causing it to function improperly. Irregular eating patterns contribute to the weight loss battle. The body tends to hoard energy in the form of fat when it doesn't know when it will be nourished again. The body responds well to regular nourishment.

My Previous Experiences With Eating Regularly

Write down your experiences with eating regularly.

My Feelings About These Experiences

Write down your feelings about these experiences.

Suggested Exercises

1. Maintain a regular eating routine: shortly after you awaken, mid-morning, lunch, mid-afternoon and evening. If you find that you're not hungry when it's time, check again in a few minutes. If you're truly not hungry, don't eat.
2. If eating a complete meal is not possible, consider eating a healthy snack, such as fruit or yogurt.
3. Refrain from overeating because you know you won't have time to eat the next meal. Make time to fuel your body!

Exploring My Understanding

Complete the following sentence: To me, *eating regularly* means . . .

Considering My Options

Complete the following sentence: NOW I'm going to . . .

EATING ONLY WHEN I'M HUNGRY

There are probably more than a dozen reasons why we eat. We eat because it's time, food's in front of us or it just looks good. We eat because we're celebrating a special occasion, we're visiting with friends or it's a holiday. We eat because it's expected, we're bored or we're emotionally upset. You can probably identify other reasons we eat, too.

One of the reasons people are not happy with their body weight is that they eat at times other than when they are truly hungry. The purpose of eating is to refuel and nourish the body so that it'll have the energy to do its work.

When we don't eat enough food, we put additional stress on the body because it must look for sources of energy that are in scarce supply. When inadequate refueling becomes a habit, the body begins to build up reserves of energy in the form of fat cells because it doesn't know when it will receive its next supply. When we eat too much food, we put additional stress on the body because it has to work more aggressively to process the excessive food. If the excess isn't eliminated through the elimination system, bodily functions are slowed and the excess is stored in fat reserves. Too much of even healthy foods is too much. Eating only when you're hungry and stopping before you're full are the most beneficial guidelines to follow.

My Previous Experiences With Eating Only When I'm Hungry

Write down your experiences with eating only when you're hungry.

My Feelings About These Experiences

Write down your feelings about these experiences.

Suggested Exercises

1. When you're feeling hungry, take a few moments to sit quietly and ask your body if it is truly hungry. If the answer is unclear, drink some water and continue with your activity. After about 15 minutes, if the hunger is apparent, ask your body again if it's hungry. When you get a clear signal that you're hungry, then eat slowly savoring each bite until you are almost full. Avoid the stuffed feeling which indicates you've overeaten.
2. If you're in the habit of eating because you're bored, look for substitutes for snacking. Instead of eating, consider stretching, taking a walk outside or a change of activity.

3. If you're in the habit of eating when you're emotional-
    ly upset or stressed out, again look for substitutes.
    Instead of eating, consider writing your thoughts down,
    calling a friend or doing a relaxation exercise.

Exploring My Understanding

Complete the following sentence: To me, *eating only when
I'm hungry* means . . .

Considering My Options

Complete the following sentence: NOW I'm going to . . .

EATING THE FOODS MY BODY LIKES

As survivors of indigestion and heartburn, we eat a lot of
foods our bodies don't like very much. Each body is unique in
this respect because a food that irritates one stomach may not
have any negative effect on another's.

The typical response to eating food that disagrees with us
is to take something to suppress the symptoms. Then we forget about the heartburn or indigestion until we have a similar
reaction. Then we repeat the cycle by taking something to give
us temporary relief.

If you listen to your body while you're eating, there's no
need for artificial means to deal with the symptoms. If you hear
that your body doesn't like particular foods or particular

combinations of foods, then you can make conscious choices about eating them again.

My Previous Experiences With Eating The Foods My Body Likes

Write down your experiences with eating the foods your body likes.

My Feelings About These Experiences

Write down your feelings about these experiences.

Suggested Exercise

When you eat a food or a combination of foods that don't digest well, reflect on what those foods are and the circumstances surrounding that snack or meal. Use this process for increasing your awareness about the foods your body doesn't like:

1. Identify the food(s) you ate. You may want to keep a record of the foods that cause you discomfort.
2. Look at the circumstances under which you were eating. Situations involving stress, alcohol and on-the-run eating will decrease the body's ability to digest your food properly.
3. Make a plan. "The next time I have the option of choosing . . . I'll choose something else" or "I'll eat only when I'm feeling calm."

4. Resolve to follow your plan. However, if you forget the
    unpleasant experience with a particular food, your
    body will remind you. Then start the process over. Your
    body will continue to remind you until you've learned
    what it likes and doesn't like.

Exploring My Understanding

Complete the following sentence: To me, *eating the foods
my body likes* means . . .

Considering My Options

Complete the following sentence: NOW I'm going to . . .

EATING A VARIETY OF FOODS

We are creatures of habit. We tend to eat the same foods
whether we're at home or eating out. We feel we've not had a
meal unless there's meat in the center of the plate. Although
we've heard all of our lives that we need to eat a variety of
foods, we don't do it because we like to eat what's familiar,
convenient and fast.

We don't like to take risks with food. But our bodies function much more efficiently when we feed them with a variety
of foods. The variety gives our bodies the myriad of nutrients
they need in the form of carbohydrates, proteins, fats, vitamins,
minerals and amino acids. When we feed our bodies limited

sources of foods, deficiencies in certain elements will likely occur. These deficiencies create added stress in the body forcing it to work harder with fewer resources.

Eating a variety of foods makes eating more interesting and offers us different experiences. Not only do we learn how the food tastes, we can also learn about the origin of the food. Because our world is a global market we have opportunities to sample many foods that were unknown to us as children. Have you ever experienced taro root, bok choy, kiwi, amaranth or white eggplant? Nutritionists recommend we eat a variety of foods including fruits, vegetables, whole grains and legumes.

My Previous Experiences With Eating A Variety Of Foods

Write down your experiences with eating a variety of foods.

My Feelings About These Experiences

Write down your feelings about these experiences.

Suggested Exercises

To increase the variety of foods you eat, experiment!

1. Make a visit to a local farmers market. Walk around and examine the different foods that are available. Ask questions about their origin, tastes and preparation. Frequently, there will be signs that indicate which familiar foods they taste like. If possible, sample them right there in the market.

2. Introduce at least one new food to your family each week. Select a new food. Find a simple recipe that high-lights its flavor. Ask a friend how he prepares it. When you eat the new food, eat it slowly savoring each bite. Enjoy your new taste experience.

3. Patronize ethnic restaurants for a new food experience. Sampling appetizers is a way to enjoy a variety of tastes. If each member of your party orders a different entree, you can enjoy an even wider variety of new foods. Remember to eat slowly and savor each bite.

Exploring My Understanding

Complete the following sentence. To me, *eating a variety of foods* means . . .

Considering My Options

Complete the following sentence: NOW I'm going to . . .

EATING BREAKFAST

There are many reasons why we don't eat breakfast. There are those related to time: "I don't have time," "I'd rather sleep" or "I'll miss the bus." Then there's "I'm not hungry," "I only need coffee to start my day" and "Who can look at food first thing in the morning?" Breakfast is the most important meal of the day because you are literally "breaking the fast" that your body's been experiencing since you last ate.

If you eat your evening meal around six o'clock and you get up at six in the morning, your body has received no new fuel for the day's work. While you sleep, your body is busy working to repair the damage you did to it during the day. It's recovering from the stresses and strains you've felt. It's regenerating new cells. Because your energy resources have been used for repair work, your body needs new reservoirs of energy to meet the demands of the new day.

It is recommended that the foods you eat at breakfast be rich in carbohydrates (whole grain breads and cereals along with fruits.) These foods supply quick energy to your system.

My Previous Experiences With Eating Breakfast

Write down your experiences with eating breakfast.

My Feelings About These Experiences

Write down your feelings about these experiences.

Suggested Exercises

1. If you do not eat breakfast now, begin by getting up 15 minutes earlier and enjoying a glass of fruit juice. Once you're use to drinking the juice, add whole grain toast or cereal. Then add a fruit or substitute the fruit for the juice.

2. For variety, make a fruit shake by mixing two or three types of fruit (a banana is usually good to add for thickness) in a blender along with a pinch of cinnamon. You can add a little carob powder, a teaspoon of nut butter, or a touch of molasses or honey if you prefer a sweeter drink.

3. Avoid coffee, doughnuts and sweet rolls at the office. They add no nutritive value to your system. Take fruit with you to work for a healthy snack. Your body will greatly appreciate your doing so!

4. If you really enjoy eggs and bacon or sausage for breakfast, save that meal for a once-in-a-while occasion.

Exploring My Understanding

Complete the following sentence: To me, *eating breakfast* means . . .

Considering My Options

Complete the following sentence: NOW I'm going to . . .

DRINKING WATER

Water is an essential substance for our bodies. Approximately two-thirds of the body is made up of water. The body needs water to replenish the cells, keep the organs and tissues supple, reduce water retention, lubricate joints, cool the body during exercise, replenish body fluids and aid the digestive and elimination systems.

Although we're a society that drinks a lot of liquids, we have many reasons for not drinking sufficient amounts of water. We don't like the taste. It contains too many chemicals and it's boring to drink. We're also unsure how much water we really need to drink. We know drinking water is good for us, yet we choose other liquids when our bodies really want and need water.

My Previous Experiences With Drinking Water

Write down your experiences with drinking water.

My Feelings About These Experiences

Write down your feelings about these experiences.

Suggested Exercises

1. To determine how much water your body needs, take your body weight and divide it by two. Your answer is the number of ounces of water your body needs daily. (Example: 150 lbs ÷ 2 = 75 oz.)

2. Rather than tap water, drink bottled spring water or mineral water. These have a more pleasant taste since they contain fewer chemicals than most tap water. Be sure to read the labels for ingredients. You may also

want to check the source of the water to be sure you're getting what you're paying for. You can also use a filtering system in your home. Total water system filters and faucet filters are available. Find a way that works for you.

3. Consider adding a slice of lemon, lime or orange to your water. Drinking water may be more palatable with this splash of flavor.

4. To substitute water for other liquids you're accustomed to drinking, have a special glass or container for water. The specialness of the container will add to the emotional comfort of adding more water to your diet.

5. To keep track of the number of ounces of water you're drinking, measure the number of ounces in the glass or container you generally drink from. Put a piece of tape on the glass and mark it each time you fill it up.

6. Chart your progress. At the end of the day, record the number of ounces you drank. This information will let you know how you're doing.

7. Listen to your body. When you're thirsty, drink water. When you've had enough, stop.

8. Sip small amounts of water while eating. Too much water tends to interfere with the digestive process. Do what works for you.

Exploring My Understanding

Complete the following sentence: To me, *drinking water* means . . .

Considering My Options

Complete the following sentence: NOW I'm going to . . .

LIMITING FATS

Excessive dietary fat, particularly the saturated kind, is linked to heart disease, obesity and a number of other health problems. Excessive fat forces the system to work harder when breaking down the fats used by the body.

Typically the foods we enjoy eating, such as ice cream, potato chips and hamburgers are high in saturated fat. Saturated fats come from animal products and tropical oils (coconut, palm and cottonseed). Fats are what make foods taste so good. Think about that choice cut of steak on the grill; the fat is what gives it its flavor.

Although the body needs fats as an energy source, to lubricate the system and to protect the organs, it doesn't need as much as we give it. Nutritionists recommend that our fat intake be less than 30 percent of the total amount of food we ingest. Each gram of fat has nine calories and is hard for our bodies to break down into usable nutrients. What our bodies don't use and don't eliminate are stored in fat cells.

When you choose fats for cooking and seasoning your meals, choose monosaturated fats, such as olive and canola oil and polyunsaturated fats, such as safflower and sunflower oil.

My Previous Experiences With Limiting Fats

Write down your experiences with limiting your fats.

My Feelings About These Experiences

Write down your feelings about these experiences.

Suggested Exercises

1. Read the labels of the food you eat. Pay attention to both the percentage of fat and the number of fat grams contained in the food. Keep in mind that all calories are not alike: Fat takes more calories to burn into energy. To illustrate this, multiply the percentage of fat grams in a food item by nine calories which will tell you how many calories it takes to burn the fat in the food. Consider eating foods with five grams of fat or less.

2. Experiment preparing and seasoning foods with different types of fat. What could you put on a baked potato other than butter? Different oils give foods different flavors. How does olive oil affect the taste of your stir-fried vegetables? How about toasted sesame oil? Keep in mind that saturated fats harden when they are at room temperature. Avoid them!

3. Rather than pouring salad dressing on your salad, put the dressing on the side and add it to your salad as you desire it. Stick your fork into the dressing, then pick up the bite of food you want to eat. You'll use less fat and get a better taste of the food you're eating.

4. Use sauces that are vegetable-based such as tomato or potato rather cream-based.

5. Whether eating out or eating in, avoid foods that are fried, sauteed in butter and covered in cream-sauce. Choose foods that are prepared with no or small amounts of fat. Foods can be prepared with little or no fat when they are boiled, steamed, broiled, grilled, baked, mircrowaved or stir-fried.

Exploring My Understanding

Complete the following sentence: To me, *limiting fats* means . . .

Considering My Options

Complete the following sentence: NOW I'm going to . . .

LIMITING CHOLESTEROL

Cholesterol is a soft fat-like substance essential to the body's functioning. It is manufactured by the liver and is found in foods derived from animals. Experts recommend that our cholesterol levels be below 200 with a higher ratio of high-density lipoproteins (HDLs) than low-density lipoproteins (LDLs). HDLs carry cholesterol away from the blood vessel walls to the liver. LDLs stick to the artery walls. The build-up in the arteries restricts the regular flow of the bloodstream which transports nutrients to the body. Excessive cholesterol is linked to heart disease, specifically atherosclerosis.

My Previous Experiences With Limiting Cholesterol

Write down your experiences with limiting cholesterol.

My Feelings About These Experiences

Write down your feelings about these experiences.

Suggested Exercises

1. Make a list of the foods you typically eat. Highlight those that are made with animal products, including eggs, cheese and milk. Look at your diet to determine if you're eating more cholesterol than your body needs.
2. If you don't know what your cholesterol reading is, have it checked. Be sure to get a reading for the HDLs as well as the LDLs. The blood test after fasting is a more accurate evaluation of your cholesterol levels. The skin-prick method can only give you general information. If your total level is above 220, scrutinize the amount and type of fat in your diet. Make changes.
3. Experiment with alternative protein-rich foods. Add soybeans, whole grains, legumes, nuts and seeds to your diet. Many vegetables including lima beans, peas and kale are good sources of protein, too.

Exploring My Understanding

Complete the following sentence: To me, *limiting cholesterol* means . . .

Considering My Options

Complete the following sentence: NOW I'm going to . . .

LIMITING ADDED SUGAR

Sugar occurs naturally in many of our foods, particularly in our fruits and vegetables. Sugar in its natural state is an important part of our diet because it provides energy in the form of simple carbohydrates for the body's work.

Many people attribute their excessive weight, lack of proper nutritional habits and loss of will power to their "sweet tooth." There is a place for all tastes in our diet, including sweetness. We tend to overdo it by drinking sweetened carbonated drinks and eating desserts such as candy, cookies, cakes and ice cream. If too much sugar is added to a food, the food loses its natural taste. Added sugars also supply the body with "empty" calories that do not add any nutritive value for the system.

Excessive sugars are converted to fat which creates a health concern. Artificial sweeteners are poor substitutes for sugar because they are unnatural chemical additives to food. When was the last time you had a diet drink along with your piece of cake?

My Previous Experiences With Limiting Added Sugar

Write down your experiences with limiting added sugar.

My Feelings About These Experiences

Write down your feelings about these experiences.

Suggested Exercises

1. When your "sweet tooth" is calling out for gratification, choose naturally sweet foods such as fruits and fruit juices. Experiment with different types of fruit. Melons and mangoes are particularly sweet.
2. Use fruit juices and molasses for sweeteners when baking cookies or cakes.
3. Use fruit spreads to add sweetness to your breads and fruits to add sweetness to your cereals.
4. Substitute honey for table sugar. You'll need a smaller amount for the same sweetness.

Exploring My Understanding

Complete the following sentence: To me, *limiting added sugar* means . . .

Considering My Options

Complete the following sentence: NOW I'm going to . . .

LIMITING CAFFEINE

Caffeine is a stimulant drug that occurs naturally. Drinking coffee and tea are ingrained social habits. We have "coffee breaks" at work. We say to our friends or business acquaintances, "Let's get together for coffee and chat." Rarely do we say, "Let's get together for spring water (or juice)."

Caffeine stimulates the body's system, temporarily creating stress for the body in addition to that desired burst of energy. The inevitable drop in energy comes shortly after. To maintain the energy boost, we have to continue ingesting caffeine. Chocolate candy bars are great for a few minutes, then . . . crash.

Caffeine is found in some very obvious places such as coffee, leaf tea, colas, chocolate and cocoa. It's also found in a number of light-colored soft drinks (Mellow Yellow and Mountain Dew) and over-the-counter diet aids. (The logic is this: caffeine stimulates the system; the system is more energetic; then more calories are burned up.)

Excessive use of caffeine has been linked to a number of side effects including birth defects, headaches, constipation and sleep problems.

My Previous Experiences With Limiting Caffeine

Write down your experiences with limiting caffeine.

My Feelings About These Experiences

Write down your feelings about these experiences.

Suggested Exercises

1. Keep a record of the foods and drinks you're ingesting that contain caffeine. Make note of how you feel 15 minutes, 30 minutes and an hour after you've finished the drink or food. You may also want to monitor your sleep and resting habits. Are you dropping off to sleep quickly? Are you waking refreshed? After a week, take a look at the information you've collected. How does your body feel and respond to the amount of caffeine ingested? Do you want to make any changes?

2. Look for caffeine substitutes. Drink hot and cold herbal tea in place of leaf teas. There is no caffeine in herbs. Use carob products in place of cocoa and chocolate products. Drink juices, sparkling waters and spritzers (fruit juices and carbonated water) for refreshment. There are a number of products on the market that are "caffeine-free." Keep in mind that most foods are naturally "caffeine-free."

Exploring My Understanding

Complete the following sentence: To me, *limiting caffeine* means . . .

Considering My Options

Complete the following sentence: NOW I'm going to . . .

AVOIDING ADDITIVES AND PRESERVATIVES

Additives and preservatives are chemical substances that have been created to make food look better, taste better and last longer. Because we are visual people, we tend to buy the foods and drinks that are visually pleasing. How often have we said, "What looks good on the menu?" So additives are added to our foods to make them look better. We're always looking for ways to make our foods taste better, so additives are used to enhance the flavor of our food, too. Due to our practical nature, we want to purchase foods that have a long shelf life, foods that don't spoil easily. So preservatives are added to our foods allowing them to last up to two to three years!

Popular additives and preservatives include monosodium glutamate (MSG) and partially hydrogenated oil, a hidden fat. These additives along with hundreds of others, make foods look good, taste good and last a very long time.

There is no nutritive benefit in additives and preservatives, and there is often a negative health reaction to them. Non-foods are very difficult for the body to break down, which creates stress on the system. If these non-foods are not eliminated through the body's elimination system, they are stored as toxins in the body. Excessive salt in the body is known to contribute significantly to high blood pressure and heart disease. Some additives have been known to create behavioral and psychological problems in adults as well as children. Aspartame, saccharin and fake fat are chemically-derived food substitutes.

My Previous Experiences With Avoiding Additives And Preservatives

Write down your experiences with avoiding additives and preservatives.

My Feelings About These Experiences

Write down your feelings about these experiences.

Suggested Exercises

1. Read the labels of packaged foods. If there are words you don't recognize or can't pronounce, they are most likely additives. Avoid products containing partially hydrogenated oils, any derivative of sodium, dyes, sulfites and anything described ". . . as a preservative."

2. When eating out in a restaurant, request that no additives be put in your food. For example, when ordering oriental food request that no MSG be used.

3. Use substitutes. If you want to enhance the flavor of your food, do so naturally with herbs and spices. There are a number of pamphlets, books and magazines that give directions on how to use herbs and spices when preparing foods. Many communities offer cooking classes about the use of herbs. There are a number of salt and seasoning substitutes. Be sure to read the label. The product may be a salt substitute and still have sodium in it. Remember if there are words on the label that you're unfamiliar with, check their meanings before putting the product in your body.

4. Eat foods that are fresh and can be seasoned naturally with herbs, spices, onions, mushrooms and monosaturated and polyunsaturated oils. The fresher the food, the more active the nutrients are that can be used by the body.

Exploring My Understanding

Complete the following sentence: To me, *avoiding additives and preservatives* means . . .

Considering My Options

Complete the following sentence: NOW I'm going to . . .

EATING FIBER

Fiber is important in the diet because it aids the elimination system in ridding the body of toxins. A number of diseases, including colon cancer, can be prevented when a sufficient amount of fiber is ingested by the body.

There are two types of fiber, soluble and insoluble. The insoluble fiber, such as the bran from whole grains, passes through the body's system taking the by-products of the digestive system with it. Soluble fiber, the type often found in fruits and vegetables, is used by the body to aid digestion and affect blood cholesterol levels.

Fibrous foods are plentiful in our society. By maintaining a healthy diet, we get the amount of fiber our body needs. The recommended standard amount of fiber is approximately 45 grams. It's important to keep in mind that our bodies are unique, requiring more or less than the standard.

Fiber can be found in foods that are plant-based, including fruits and vegetables, whole grains, legumes and nuts. Some of the foods containing significant amounts of fiber (7 grams or more) include black beans, kidney beans, pinto beans, broccoli, avocado, green peas, spinach, blackberries, dried figs (without sulfites), prunes, plums, raspberries and watermelon. Meats, seafood, fish, dairy products, oils and sugar contain no fiber.

My Previous Experiences With Eating Fiber

Write down your experiences with eating fiber.

My Feelings About These Experiences

Write down your feelings about these experiences.

Suggested Exercises

1. Make a list of the foods you eat on a regular basis. Put them in categories: FIBER and NON-FIBER. If you have an overwhelming number of foods in the non-fiber category, think about what foods you can add to your diet or eliminate so you have a better balance.
2. Read labels to determine the amount of fiber contained in products you purchase. If the amount is less than 2 or 3 grams, then the fiber content is negligible.
3. Eat whole foods. Much of the fiber is often destroyed when foods are processed. Steaming sometimes adds a very small amount of fiber to vegetables.

4. Drink plenty of water! If you don't drink enough water, you'll likely find your self constipated.
5. Refrain from overdoing it! Listen to your body, and monitor your bowel movements. Eating too much fiber can clog up the large intestine causing constipation.

Exploring My Understanding

Complete the following sentence: To me, *eating fiber* means . . .

Considering My Options

Complete the following sentence: NOW I'm going to . . .

MAINTAINING MY IDEAL WEIGHT

Weight loss is a multimillion dollar industry. As a society, we seem to be obsessed with how much we weigh. Many of us "freak out" when we get on the scale and find we weigh one pound more than we did the week before. We are inundated with television, radio and print ads to lose weight suggesting to us that whatever we weigh is too much. We compare our weight to artificial standards, to our best friend, to the neighbor next door, to models, actors and to what we weighed ten years ago. There are literally hundreds of diet plans. Some have helpful information, others include practices that may be detrimental to your health. It's important for us to maintain an appropriate amount of weight, which is dependent on many things, for our bodies to function properly. Our genes, bone structure, height and metabolism all play a role in determining our appropriate weight. To maintain our "ideal" weight, we need to be in tune with our bodies. Following someone else's prescribed system of eating may or may not work for you. You have to experiment and find out what the best way is to fuel and nourish your body. Then you can make conscious choices about what's best for *your* body.

My Previous Experiences With Maintaining My Ideal Weight

Write down your experiences with maintaining your ideal weight.

My Feelings About These Experiences

Write down your feelings about these experiences.

Suggested Exercises

1. Get rid of your scales! Monitor your weight by how you feel, how your body functions and how you look to your self. Muscle weighs more than fat!
2. Exercise on a regular basis.

3. Eat foods that will fuel your body's processes and replenish the nutrients in your body. Whole foods are your best selection. The more processed the food, the fewer nutrients and more calories it contains.

4. For a week, keep a record of what you eat and why you're eating. Look at the reasons you eat. We eat for many reasons, most of which have nothing to do with being hungry. Determine your reasons and brainstorm what alternatives you have. For example, if you're eating because you need to take a break, consider stretching or taking a walk outside. If you're eating because you're upset, consider calling a friend, crying, writing your thoughts down or taking a short walk. Make a list of alternative responses you can make in the place of eating.

5. Eat only when you're truly hungry. Before you begin eating or preparing your food, take a few quiet moments, place your hand on your stomach and ask your self, "Am I really hungry?" Wait for a response, then move on. If your response is ambiguous, drink some water and ask again in about 15 minutes. Refrain from eating because others want you to or it's time.

6. Eat only when you're sitting in a calm environment. When you have a specific routine, liking sitting at the table without distraction, you're cuing your body to pre-pare for digestion. By paying attention to your food, rather than reading, watching television or engaging in debate, your body can concentrate on assimilating your food.

7. Eat slowly. After taking a bite of food, put your fork or spoon down, and rest your hand in your lap. Then enjoy the tastes that your mouth is experiencing. Feel the texture and temperature of the food. Chew your food until there is nothing left to chew, then swallow, and then take the next bite. Keep in mind that digestion begins in the mouth with the chewing process. The

more completely you chew your food, the easier it is for your body to digest it.

8. Eat and drink only the foods that agree with your body. Experiment with foods. If you eat a spicy meal and you have indigestion afterwards, consider what ingredients may have caused the indigestion. Pay closer attention to those foods the next time you eat them. If you find they continue to upset your system, eliminate them from your diet. After you know which foods don't agree with you, don't eat them!

9. Stop eating when you're almost full. It takes time (possibly up to 20 minutes) for the stomach to cue the brain that it's full. Eating slowly will give your stomach more time to send its message. Refrain from eating more than what you want. Don't give in to pressure to have one more piece or just one more bite. Remember you're not the garbage pail!

10. Eat your last meal early in the evening so your body will have time to digest the food. If you eat later in the evening, eat a lighter meal.

11. If you're hungry and in a rush, consider drinking some fruit juice until you have time to eat what your body needs in a calm and relaxing environment.

Exploring My Understanding

Complete the following sentence: To me, *maintaining my ideal weight* means . . .

Considering My Options

Complete the following sentence: NOW I'm going to . . .

ELIMINATING TOXINS

From what we eat, how we deal with our stress and our normal everyday body processes, toxins are created in our bodies. The liver's primary function is to process those toxins for elimination, which generally occurs through the kidneys, bowels, breath and skin. When those processes don't function regularly and adequately, the toxic waste products interfere with the normal functioning of the body. This creates stress on the system because the toxins will filter back into the muscles, bloodstream and cells. Then the liver has to once again process the toxins for elimination. When the liver is overworked because of excessive toxicity, it will begin to deteriorate creating a condition, cirrhosis of the liver, an eventual fatal condition. You can prevent such a travesty from occurring by paying attention to what you put in your body, reducing your stress and having a regular routine for elimination.

My Previous Experiences With Eliminating Toxins

Write down your experiences with eliminating toxins.

My Feelings About These Experiences

Write down your feelings about these experiences.

Suggested Exercises

1. Drink plenty of water. Water moves toxins through the system.
2. Treat your self to a full body massage. The process of massaging the muscles releases lactic acid that builds up in the muscles as a result of exercising and stress. Drink plenty of water after your massage! (Make sure your massage therapist is trained and licensed or certified, and is a member of the American Massage Therapy Association. The requirements for licensing are different in each state.)
3. Take a steam (wet heat) or sauna (dry heat) bath. The heat causes the body to sweat releasing toxins through the skin. You may want to use a dry brush on your skin before you enter the room or a loofah brush while you're sweating. Both of these will remove dead skin cells from your skin, allowing your pores to open more fully. Be sure to follow the on-site directions that are associated with the use of either of these rooms. Maximum time using either room is usually 15 minutes. If this is a new experience for you, stay in for a short amount of time, whatever feels comfortable to you. You'll receive the most benefit wearing no clothing. Some type of shoes and a towel, however, are highly recommended!
4. Set aside time each day for regular bladder and bowel elimination. Because every body functions a bit differently, experiment and find what works for you. You

may want to consider sitting quietly for 15 minutes after each meal. No matter what, when nature calls, respond! You interfere with your system's functioning when you delay your response.

5. Consider having a "fruit day" when you eat only fruit or drink fruit juices and water to soothe your system and to get rid of toxins. Fruits are generally processed by the body in about 30 minutes, they contain some fiber, and they act as cleansing agents for the system.

6. Avoid laxatives. Most laxatives chemically and artificially induce bowel movements. This chemical inducement interferes with the body's ability to function properly.

7. Eat a healthy diet, including adequate fiber.

Exploring My Understanding

Complete the following sentence: To me, *eliminating toxins* means . . .

Considering My Options

Complete the following sentence: NOW I'm going to . . .

DRINKING ALCOHOL IN MODERATION

If we choose to drink alcohol, we need to make conscious choices about doing so. There are a number of reasons we choose to drink alcohol. We've had a hard day. It's a habit. It's available. It's expected. We're celebrating. We're with friends. We're overwhelmed. It's a holiday. And in the most serious case, we're addicted. Keep in mind that alcohol is a toxin.

Beer and wine have limited nutritional value. The caloric content is usually referred to as "empty" calories because the alcohol does not refuel and nourish the body. Those empty calories are stored in fat cells. When we drink, we add stress to the body's functions. The liver must work overtime to process the toxins in the alcohol. Our mental clarity is decreased because alcohol enters the bloodstream quickly. Toxins in the body slow bodily functions, dull the senses, lengthen reaction time and can lead to serious life-threatening diseases.

A number of research studies have been conducted to evaluate the benefits of drinking in moderation. Generally, the results indicate that those subjects (usually males) who drink alcohol in moderation (defined as two drinks per day, one per hour) tend to live longer and healthier lives than those who never drink and those who have a problem with alcohol consumption. You need to be acutely aware of the reasons you drink as you listen to your body's reaction to your alcohol consumption.

My Previous Experiences With Drinking Alcohol In Moderation

Write down your experiences with drinking alcohol in moderation.

My Feelings About These Experiences

Write down your feelings about these experiences.

Suggested Exercises

1. Determine your reasons for drinking alcohol. If you drink because you want to escape from your problems and concerns, GET HELP. Talking to a trusted friend when you're feeling overwhelmed is a more effective way of dealing with your concerns. Counseling is also available through health plans, community agencies, private practices, religious institutions and out-patient hospital programs. Ask your friends or professionals for recommendations or check the Yellow Pages of your telephone directory.

2. If you've ever had a problem with alcohol, refrain from drinking.

3. If you choose to drink, do so in moderation. Researchers consider moderation to be no more than two drinks a day. You must decide for your self what moderation means to you.

4. Refrain from operating machinery, including your car, when you are drinking.

5. If you drink, also eat. Food absorbs the alcohol and slows its entry into the bloodstream.

6. Closely monitor your behavior and feelings about drinking. Listen to your body's response to ingesting alcohol. If you have a hang-over or become sick to your stomach, decrease the amount and frequency of your drinking.

7. Make a conscious choice to drink. Whether or not you choose to drink is entirely up to you.

Exploring My Understanding

Complete the following sentence: To me, *drinking alcohol in moderation* means . . .

Considering My Options

Complete the following sentence: NOW I'm going to . . .

REFRAINING FROM SMOKING

There is no health benefit from smoking for the smoker or for others exposed to the smoke. Nicotine is a drug that poisons the body. It's an addictive substance that enslaves thousands of people, young and old, rich and poor. Smoking begins as an experiment, a way to belong, a way to calm one's nerves, and then it becomes a habit and an addiction.

Lung cancer is one of the leading causes of illness and death in our society. Illness and cancer from secondary smoke is a major health concern. If you smoke, you're robbing your self of years of life and dooming your self and others to disease and premature death.

My Previous Experiences With Refraining From Smoking

Write down your experiences with refraining from smoking.

My Feelings About These Experiences

Write down your feelings about these experiences.

Suggested Exercises

1. Look at your reasons for smoking. Determine what the advantages and disadvantages are for you. Determine what the advantages and disadvantages are for others. Consider how you would benefit by giving up smoking. Consider how others would benefit.
2. Make a list of when you smoke and the surrounding circumstances. Look for the triggers, such as when you're drinking coffee during a break, when you're having a drink with friends, when you're nervous about an interview. Recognizing the triggers will make you aware of your reasons and times that you smoke.
3. Make a conscious choice to stop smoking. Any habit can be changed. You have to decide that being a nonsmoker is something you passionately desire to do.
4. Frequently take a few quiet moments to relax in a comfortable position. Visualize your self not smoking in situations where you're accustomed to smoking. When a cigarette is offered to you, imagine your self with brilliant colors and the sound of your voice saying, "No, thank you. I'm a nonsmoker." Smell the cleanness of the air around you. Taste the flavors of the foods you eat. Feel the confidence you have in your self for taking control over your life. Bring this picture of your self as a nonsmoker into your awareness every time you feel the urge to smoke. Rather than smoking, take that three to five minutes to picture your self as a nonsmoker. Find substitutes for smoking: chew gum, take deep

breaths, do some stretching exercises or hold a pencil or straw in your hands. Think of your self as a non-smoker. Say to your self frequently, "I'm a nonsmoker." Make visual reminders that you're a nonsmoker.

5. If you find it difficult to stop smoking on your own, consider enrolling in a smoking cessation program. Check out the success rate of the program before making an investment in it. If the program can't give you enough information, look elsewhere. Ask other former smokers about methods they used to quit smoking. Some hypnotherapists have acted as change agents for smokers who wanted to quit. If you want to investigate using the hypnosis process, look for a licensed hypnotherapist. Ask about their experience with smokers. Ask for references. Some clients have been known to stop after only one hypnosis session. For others, they've needed more sessions. Keep in mind your own response will vary. Whatever method you choose, make sure you feel comfortable with it. Do what works for you!

Exploring My Understanding

Complete the following sentence: To me, *refraining from smoking* means . . .

Considering My Options

Complete the following sentence: NOW I'm going to . . .

8
Growing InSync with the Social Dimension

With the knowledge we acquired from making a substantial investment of our time, energy and resources in our selves, we open the passageways for opportunities to effectively nurture and support the other people in our lives. We find that this knowledge prepares us for understanding, relating and communicating with others. It is in developing, nurturing and maintaining healthy relationships that we continue to grow and seek out what we truly want in life.

Relationships are developed with compatible purposes in mind. They are most often silent agreements to seek out opportunities to help one another get what he or she wants. The extent of that help varies according to the type of relationship, its level of intensity and the nature of the involvement.

A relationship is a complex entity because each of us brings to it our own unique view of the world which affects all of our thoughts, feelings and actions. No one relationship can be designed to meet all of our needs and fulfill all of our desires, so it's important to nurture and maintain a number of relationships that give us enjoyment.

Maintaining relationships enable us to strengthen the connection we feel with others. By giving and receiving support, by communicating openly and by consciously cooperating, we give others the opportunity to grow, develop and get what they want out of life, too.

The maintenance of a relationship is a process that brings with it many challenges and many pleasures. When we treat others with dignity and respect, we support them in their endeavor to make life what they want it to be. Although allowing others to find their own way is difficult, it's imperative that we let them learn the lessons that come from making one's own mistakes.

There are many ways we can give to others. Your caring and your actions can significantly impact the lives of others as well as your own. Be ever mindful that it's because we have given to our selves that we can give to others.

Using the social dimension exercises, we'll explore ways of communicating openly, cooperating consciously, receiving and giving support, enjoying life and physical contact, treating others with dignity and respect and getting what you want from others.

Please refer to page 40 for directions on how to maximize your experiences.

VALUING OTHERS

Just as you are unique, unrepeatable and of precious worth, so is every other person. Although we often disagree with others' ideas, thoughts, feelings and behaviors, they still deserve to be valued and respected. We need to keep in mind that true value is intrinsic and unrelated to everything else about the person. How others feel, think and respond to the world around them is a direct reflection of how they value them selves. By recognizing that every individual has gifts and talents to share, we validate their value. We can offer encouragement to others so that they find the strength to see their own inherent worth and use their talents and gifts.

Valuing is very difficult because we're inhibited by past experiences and preconceived notions about others. Moving beyond these self-created limitations is significant for your growth and development.

My Previous Experiences With Valuing Others

Write down your experiences with valuing others.

My Feelings About These Experiences:

Write down your feelings about these experiences.

Suggested Exercise

In the center of separate sheets of paper, write the names of three people with whom you have a very close relationship. Think about what you value and consider precious about each one of them. Use whatever format works for you and express your feelings and thoughts on the paper. Using the same process, select three people with whom you have unresolved conflicts. Identify what brings value to their lives and how you feel about relating to them as a result of what you've discovered during this process.

Exploring My Understanding

Complete the following sentence: To me, *valuing others* means . . .

Considering My Options

Complete the following sentence: NOW I'm going to . . .

TREATING OTHERS WITH DIGNITY AND RESPECT

The Golden Rule directs us to treat others as we want to be treated. Perhaps another interpretation is that we need to treat others with dignity and respect. When we treat others with dignity, we don't act in any way that would undermine their feelings about themselves or negatively influence the feelings others have about them. When we treat others with respect, we recognize their rights to be, feel, do and think whatever they want, even when those ideas, feelings and actions don't necessarily agree with our own.

This is a tough task to tackle. It's easy to have that warm fuzzy feeling about people who are like us. When people differ from us, particularly on basic fundamental issues, we reject them as well as their ideas and actions.

Treating others with dignity and respect isn't about that warm fuzzy feeling, nor is it about being friends. You can respect others without developing a meaningful relationship. Treating others with dignity and respect is about honoring the differences among us. It's about giving others freedom to be and do whatever they choose.

When we don't treat others with dignity and respect, we're passing judgment on them. We're saying that they're not good enough. We're saying that in order to be accepted, they're going to have to change their ways and their thinking. Many of us are familiar with not meeting someone else's standards. We know what it's like not being good enough to be accepted and how it affects every part of our life. It behooves us to refrain from creating any conditions in which others will experience those feelings of inadequacy and poor self-worth.

How we treat others says a lot more about us than it does about them. So if you treat your self with dignity and respect and expect others to do so, then you're more likely to do the same with others.

My Previous Experiences With Treating Others With Dignity And Respect

Write down your experiences with treating others with dignity and respect.

My Feelings About These Experiences

Write down your feelings about these experiences.

Suggested Exercise

At the end of the day, think about how you treated others: your loved ones, your co-workers, the homeless person asking for money or work, the grocery store clerk at the checkout counter, the physically challenged co-worker who's wheelchair slowed your pace down in the hallway, the cleaning crew in your office building, the parking lot attendant, the oversized lady on the bus, train or plane, the person who pulled out in front of you in traffic, or the receptionist that transposed the numbers in a telephone number. Ask your self these questions: *How would you feel if you had been in their position and were treated by someone else as you treated them? Do you want to make any changes in the way you acted toward another? What can you do differently the next time you encounter that person?*

One way to begin revising your perspective about others when you encounter them is to say to your self, "I affirm your value and worthiness."

Exploring My Understanding

Complete the following sentence: To me, *treating others with dignity and respect* means . . .

Considering My Options

Complete the following sentence: NOW I'm going to . . .

LOVING OTHERS UNCONDITIONALLY

Loving others unconditionally is possible when we love our selves without condition. Unconditional love means we cherish others without our expectations or conditions being met. We all know conditional love too well. We've heard it with "When you do what I expect you to, then I'll love you" and "If you'll change your ways, then I'll love you." The conditional love and acceptance we have experienced throughout our lives has created havoc for us. We're always trying to meet others expectations and denying our own individuality.

Loving unconditionally means you love regardless of, and sometimes in spite of, any action, thought or feeling the other person may or may not demonstrate or possess. It means you love during the pleasant times as well as the difficult ones. It means you don't give up on that person and you support him or her emotionally with your love. Loving unconditionally means you don't disengage your self from a relationship because that person didn't meet your expectations. Keep in mind that the more you love your self without conditions, the more you understand the value of loving others unconditionally.

My Previous Experiences With Loving Others Unconditionally

Write down your experiences with loving others unconditionally.

My Feelings About These Experiences

Write down your feelings about these experiences.

Suggested Exercise

Write the names of those you love across the top of separate pieces of paper. Use as many sheets as you need. Now think about each one individually. What are the conditions each person must meet in order for you to fully share your love with them? Think about those conditions. Are you willing to withdraw these conditions from the relationship? What can you do to eliminate them? How can you move beyond these conditions in this relationship? To make this task manageable, address one relationship at a time. This will avoid the overwhelming feeling that is likely to surface with this emotionally-charged task.

Exploring My Understanding

Complete the following sentence: To me, *loving others unconditionally* means . . .

Considering My Options

Complete the following sentence: NOW I'm going to . . .

SUPPORTING OTHERS

When someone asks you for a listening ear or emotional support, even someone you don't know very well, what is your natural inclination? Most of the time, we'll listen or give words of encouragement because we naturally like to help people. We receive pleasure from being a support to others. We offer support because it makes us feel important, gives us value and worth, reflects positively on us and gives us a way to use our time, energy and resources in a productive way.

We also offer support because we've been told throughout our lives that if we take care of others they will take care of us. So sometimes our motivation for giving support is selfish rather than altruistic. We sometimes believe that giving support to others means that we take responsibility for seeing that their needs are met and then expect that they will be responsible for seeing that our needs are met in return. When we truly give support to others, we expect nothing in return, and we don't take responsibility for their situation. Giving support, particularly of the emotional nature, lets the person know that you're in their corner no matter what the outcome of their situation might be.

My Previous Experiences With Supporting Others

Write down your experiences with supporting others.

My Feelings About These Experiences

Write down your feelings about these experiences.

Suggested Exercise

Identify those people for whom you provide an emotional support on a rather frequent basis. When your friends are not in an emotional crisis, ask them if they'd participate in a mini-survey. Pose the following questions to them:

- How can I improve the way I provide support to you?
- What do I do that feels supportive?
- What do I do that interferes with the emotional support you feel?
- Is there anything you want me to stop doing?
- Do you feel I'm there for you during your time of need rather than seeking what I can get out of the situation?

It may seem strange to conduct a survey with your friends about how you provide support. By doing so, it'll let your friends know you're serious about giving them the type of emotional support they need when they seek you out for help. It's recommended that you approach one friend at a time for this exercise. Keep in mind that the responses you receive may vary widely because each of your friends is an individual.

Exploring My Understanding

Complete the following sentence: To me, *supporting others* means . . .

Considering My Options

Complete the following sentence: NOW I'm going to . . .

ALLOWING OTHERS TO FOLLOW THEIR OWN PATH

Others often seek our assistance in a matter that is perplexing to them. After hearing about the specifics, we frequently compare their dilemma to ones we've experienced. We erroneously think they want us to tell them how to deal with the situation. Many times what they want and need is a nonjudging listening ear of someone who can be a partner in an open discussion. Since we're often familiar with their talents, skills, past experience and the way they deal best with situations, we believe we know what's best for them. We're confident that if they would only take a certain course of action their dilemma would be resolved. We're quick to encourage them to move along the path of *our* choosing.

When we truly care about others and want to provide them with emotional support, we must let them follow their own path. With every experience we go where no other human being has traveled. We must be emotionally committed and believe our actions are the best ones for us. If we attempt to meet others' expectations, then we're not truly living our lives. Keep in mind there's no one right path to anywhere. Everyone must seek out what works best for them.

So when someone comes to you for assistance, offer what they need most—an unrelenting listener, a sounding board for their ideas and a catalyst for their development. Only if they ask, help them brainstorm for possible solutions, weighing the advantages and disadvantages of implementing each solution. Most importantly, help others be involved in the process of becoming themselves. Give them the freedom to take responsibility for their lives and respond to situations in the ways they feel will be in their own best interest.

My Previous Experiences With Allowing Others To Follow Their Own Path

Write down your experiences with allowing others to follow their own path.

My Feelings About These Experiences

Write down your feelings about these experiences.

Suggested Exercise

When a friend approaches you for assistance with a challenging situation, ask them what type of assistance they need before you plunge in with advice on how to remedy the situation. If you're not clear what they want from you, continue to ask questions until you are. Gently remind your friend that they are responsible for the outcome, and that you can only be responsible for listening and stimulating their thoughts. Assure your friend with support in making whatever decision they feel is best for them. Keep in mind that their choices may differ from what you'd select for them and that's completely acceptable to you! (This part will be tough—you can do it!) If you're asked for something you can't give, let your friend know up front. Refrain from making promises you can't deliver.

Exploring My Understanding

Complete the following sentence: To me, *allowing others to follow their own path* means . . .

Considering My Options

Complete the following sentence: NOW I'm going to . . .

GIVING TO OTHERS

Giving to others who find themselves in less fortunate circumstances than we're in is an important way to share our talents and skills. There are many benefits for us when we give to others freely without compensation. Some of those benefits include learning more about human nature, getting to know our selves better, developing a better understanding of others and using our time, energy and resources to make a contribution to our communities.

We may find that the greatest benefit of all is the joy we receive in giving. Just as when we give to our selves we have more to give to others, when we give to others we also have more to give to our selves. Wherever we find our selves in life, we know there are those who are in situations that are less than comfortable. What a great contribution we can make when we share willingly and selflessly what we have with others!

My Previous Experiences With Giving To Others

Write down your experiences with giving to others.

My Feelings About These Experiences

Write down your feelings about these experiences.

Suggested Exercise

Get involved as a volunteer with an association in your community that targets a population of interest to you, such as the Council on Child Abuse, Big Brothers/Big Sisters or the American Cancer Society. Talk with the volunteer placement coordinator to find out what types of opportunities are available. Determine what skills you can offer to help meet their needs. Take part in the training program that is offered. (Many associations require that you participate in the training. Training programs are generally designed to acquaint you with the association, the work they do, their targeted population, procedures and any skills you may need to learn).

Make a commitment to the recipients of your efforts, to the association and to your self that you'll volunteer for a designated amount of time. At the end of that time, determine if this is the type of volunteer work for you. If it is, recommit. If you feel your skills can be used more effectively in another situation, then seek it out. From time to time, reflect on the benefits of your service to others. (There are literally thousands of associations that seek volunteers each year. For more ideas, look in the Yellow Pages, talk with others in your community or contact your local United Way agency.)

Exploring My Understanding

Complete the following sentence: To me, *giving to others* means . . .

Considering My Options

Complete the following sentence: NOW I'm going to . . .

RECEIVING SUPPORT FROM OTHERS

While giving support to others is generally something we receive pleasure from doing, we are reluctant to seek support. We often feel we're burdening another person by sharing our dilemma with them. We're concerned that some of the messages we're sending to others may include "I can't handle things my self," "I'm not as strong as you thought I was," "I'm not self sufficient," "I don't have all of the answers" or "I'm not as smart as I lead other people to believe I am." We're also reluctant to seek support from others because it increases our propensity to feel insecure because we don't know everything we need to about every situation. We may fear that our request for help may be rejected. While that's possible, the rejection is not necessarily a rejection of you as a person. It may be that the person you're seeking assistance from is not in a position to help you at that particular time because of his or her own situation.

When you ask for support, it is beneficial to tell the other person what it is you need from them. Do you need encouragement? Do you need suggestions? Do you need a sounding board? When you're clear in telling others what you need, then they'll feel more comfortable to assist you in getting what you want. Keep in mind that you don't relinquish responsibility for your situation when you ask for assistance. You're gaining insight and information to help you make a more effective decision.

Be selective when you request support from another, and be cognizant of what that person can give you. If you need a listening ear, don't call someone who is better at brainstorming options.

Also remember that asking for help does not devalue your own self-worth. Asking for assistance allows you to use your own skills and abilities better by making effective decisions and bringing resolution to difficult situations. Realize that your friends won't feel like you're placing a heavy burden on them. Just as you need to give others support, others need to give you support. Our need for support reaffirms the connection we have with other human beings.

My Previous Experiences With Receiving Support From Others

Write down your experiences with receiving support from others.

My Feelings About These Experiences

Write down your feelings about these experiences.

Suggested Exercise

Think about a situation you're involved with now that you have some concerns about how to handle. Ask your self these questions:

- What do I need to know more about?
- What doesn't make sense to me about the situation?
- What do I want to happen?
- What are some of the possible outcomes?
- How emotionally invested am I in this situation?
- Is there any room for compromise?

After you've taken the time to analyze the situation, then think about the people who can provide support for you. Ask your self:

- Who could help me think through the situation with a more objective viewpoint?
- What do I need from this person?
- Do I need someone to listen?
- Do I need someone who can interpret the situation a different way?
- Do I want someone who can brainstorm options with me?

Once you've decided what you need and who the best person is to help you, then contact him or her. Begin your conversation with, "I need your help" and then state how they can help you. Be certain you thank them for their investment of time, energy and resources. After your discussion, you'll have more information, insight and a broader perspective. Then you'll be in a better position to deal with your situation. You'll enjoy the benefit you receive when you allow others to provide support.

Exploring My Understanding

Complete the following sentence: To me, *receiving support from others* means . . .

Considering My Options

Complete the following sentence: NOW I'm going to . . .

COMMUNICATING OPENLY

We are communicating all of the time. We communicate with our words, the tones in our voices, gestures, sighs, our bodies and even our silence. We communicate to convey information, ideas and feelings. We communicate to solicit and clarify feedback. And we communicate to make connections with others. We consciously and unconsciously create barriers that inhibit open communication. Those barriers include our hidden agendas, ineffective listening habits, and neglectful handling of feedback.

Often, we enter into a relationship—business or personal—with a hidden agenda. We don't specifically state what we want from the relationship, and we manipulate the situation so we can get what we want.

There are times when we pretend we're listening by looking at the person or occasionally saying, "yeah" or "uh-huh," yet our minds are thinking about other things.

Sometimes we don't really listen to others because we believe we already know what they're going to say. When we prejudge, we dismiss any opportunity to openly communicate and develop a healthy relationship with another person.

Often, we just don't want to hear what the other person has to say. For some reason, many of us believe that if we listen to what another is saying, we're in essence agreeing with them. That's not the case at all! We can let the other person know that we hear what they're saying and that we don't agree, if that's the case.

Many times we give a directive to another and then we're surprised when things don't turn out the way we expected. When we neglect to solicit feedback from our communication partner, we leave the follow-through of that directive to chance. The interpretation of what is said can vary dramatically from individual to individual. So when giving directives, ask the other person to help you by confirming the directions you gave.

Creating barriers in the communication process and refusing to eliminate them inhibit the development of positive and trusting relationships. There is a purpose in entering every relationship, even if it's temporary such as purchasing food from the grocery store or helping someone fix a flat tire. All parties in the communication exchange get involved for what they can give and what they can expect to receive from the relationship. When you effectively and openly communicate, you're more likely to get what you want, and others will get what they want.

My Previous Experiences With Communicating Openly

Write down your experiences with communicating openly.

My Feelings About These Experiences

Write down your feelings about these experiences.

Suggested Exercise

On one side of a piece of paper write down the following barriers to communication: not listening, prejudging, refusing to accept the message, maintaining hidden agendas and neglecting to solicit feedback. Now note a time when you've used those barriers to stifle communication. Look at your reasons for using the barrier. Next, identify at least one way you can eliminate the barrier in your communication with others.

Exploring My Understanding

Complete the following sentence: To me, *communicating openly* means . . .

Considering My Options

Complete the following sentence: NOW I'm going to . . .

LISTENING TO OTHERS

Listening is perhaps the most critical, as well as the most difficult, communication skill to master. Genuine nonevaluative listening occurs less often than we'd like to admit.

Several things can occur when another person is speaking to us. We're second guessing what they're going to say next. We're making an evaluation of what they're saying and how they're saying it. We're thinking of how we're going to respond to their comments. We're thinking about something totally unrelated. We may even be making up our grocery list if what they're saying is not interesting to us. We begin talking just as soon as there's a break in the conversation. We don't want to be left out. We don't want to forget what we have to say. We want to press our point rather than processing what we've heard.

By not listening, we're devaluing the other person and what he or she wants to share with us. If we're really not interested in having the conversation with that person, we can demonstrate our respect for them by informing them of our disinterest. One of the greatest gifts we can give to others is to listen to them. People tend to feel better about them selves when they've vocally expressed their thoughts, opinions, feelings and concerns to someone who cares enough about them to truly listen.

My Previous Experiences With Listening To Others

Write down your experiences with listening to others.

My Feelings About These Experiences

Write down your feelings about these experiences.

Suggested Exercises

1. Monitor how effectively you listen to others. You may want to keep a log of what you were thinking when you were "listening" to someone else speak. If the information you collect is not satisfactory to you, you may want to use the following exercises to improve your skills.

2. To eliminate the urge to begin talking immediately when the other person is pausing or completing their comments, wait. Once the other person has completed making their comments, wait at least five seconds before sharing your response. When you wait, you'll have time to process the information and formulate your response. Although the silence seems uncomfortable for many people, it's a valuable tool for understanding another's remarks.

3. When you want to be supportive in your listening and you want to confirm what you heard is accurate, use rephrasing. Once the speaker has concluded his or her comments, wait. Then rephrase what you heard. You

don't have to regurgitate word-for-word. Just give the essence of the comments made. By using this technique, others will know you've been listening. You'll also have a more accurate understanding of what's being conveyed to you.

Exploring My Understanding

Complete the following sentence: To me, *listening to others* means . . .

Considering My Options

Complete the following sentence: NOW I'm going to . . .

EXPRESSING MY IDEAS

Often we feel that what we think is unimportant. We think others won't like or accept our ideas. We think that if others reject our ideas that we, too, are being rejected.

It's important for us to express our ideas. The idea you express may not be accepted in its entirety or in its original form, yet it may lead to an even better idea that will benefit you and those involved in the exchange. Sometimes it's the perceived silly idea or the one that's "off-the-wall" that serves as a springboard for a terrific idea that will make a difference in your life, the lives of others or in your company.

Keep in mind that not all good ideas come to fruition. The

timing or the circumstances might not be right for the idea to work. However, you'll never know if your idea can serve as the catalyst for the situation at hand unless you express it!

My Previous Experiences With Expressing My Ideas

Write down your experiences with expressing your ideas.

My Feelings About These Experiences

Write down your feelings about these experiences.

Suggested Exercise

When asked for your ideas, *mindstorm* before you give them to others. *Mindstorming* is an individual brainstorming technique. At the top of a page, write down the situation calling for new ideas. Then write down at least 25 ideas without evaluation. You'll then have a number of ideas you can share. When you mindstorm, you realize there are many possibilities that can be considered.

Exploring My Understanding

Complete the following sentence: To me, *expressing my ideas* means . . .

Considering My Options

Complete the following sentence: NOW I'm going to . . .

GETTING WHAT I WANT FROM OTHERS

In order to accomplish most of our goals and activities, we need the cooperation of others. And we need a method for communicating our needs and desires to them. We have the tendency to believe that we don't have the right to ask for assistance. Yet, if we don't directly communicate, the possibility of getting what we need and want is nil.

Expressing your desires is both essential and respectful. There's no course that teaches us mind reading. So if we want others to help us meet our needs and fulfill our desires, we have to communicate our intentions effectively. Often what you want from others is to listen to your ideas. Other times, you seek specific actions from them on your behalf. By letting others know specifically what you need, obtaining what you desire from them will not be left to chance. Use direct language, including "I-statements" to express your needs and desires. For example, "I want to spend Saturday afternoon with you in the park," "I want you to listen to my reasoning about this dilemma" or "I need you to pick up the children from school. I have a meeting that will run later than usual." In reality, your request for assistance without any type of explanation is sufficient reason for others to help you. It's up to you to decide if you want to give one.

Whether you give a reason or not, often depends on the circumstances and the relationship you have with another. If you give an explanation, do so because you choose to. Don't explain just because it's expected or it's a habit. You'll also want to keep in mind that just because you ask, doesn't necessarily mean you'll receive. However, if you never ask, you can be sure you won't receive.

My Previous Experiences With Getting What I Want From Others

Write down your experiences with getting what you want from others.

My Feelings About These Experiences

Write down your feelings about these experiences.

Suggested Exercise

When asking for assistance from others, keep the following in mind:

- Use "I" statements.
- State specifically what you need or want.
- Offer no explanation for your request unless you consciously choose to do so.
- Share with them whatever information they'll need in order for them to do what you've asked them to do.
- Indicate what your time frame is.
- Give them time to think about your request and respond.
- Expect a timely response.

- Be prepared for a "no" response to your request for assistance. (Remember a "no" is not a rejection of you. There may be many reasons another person can't help you. Also keep in mind that they don't have to give you an explanation for saying "no" to your request.)
- Thank them for their assistance or their willingness to consider your request.

Example: I want to spend Saturday afternoon with you in the park. I'd like to know by tomorrow noon if it's agreeable with you. Thanks for your willingness to consider my request. (This may sound a bit formal, depending on the type of relationship you have with the other person. Use words that work for you. Make sure you include all the parts.)

Exploring My Understanding

Complete the following sentence: To me, *getting what I want from others* means . . .

Considering My Options

Complete the following sentence: NOW I'm going to . . .

COMMUNICATING WITH MY BODY

Although much emphasis is put on what we say and how we say it, the vehicle that carries the true message is our bodies. The volume of the message sent by our bodies is much louder than the one conveyed by our words.

If we're talking with someone and we're saying things we don't really mean, our bodies will convey the true message— what we really want to say. We believe the message sent to us by the body. Have you ever heard the words, "I love you" and felt they were untrue?

When you have an unpleasant message to send, refrain from masking it with words that are untrue. Although it's risky, use your courage and inner strength to let the other person know what you're feeling and thinking. Awareness that our messages must be congruent for them to be received is critical. Make sure the message you intend to send is congruent with your heart and mind.

My Previous Experiences With Communicating With My Body

Write down your experiences with communicating with your body.

My Feelings About These Experiences

Write down your feelings about these experiences.

Suggested Exercise

Rather than listening only with your ears, start listening to other's comments to you with your eyes and your feelings. Watch what they do with their bodies and make note of how you feel while you're speaking with them as well as how you feel after the conversation is concluded. Reflect on your conversation: *What message were they sending with their words? What message did I receive from their bodies? How congruent is the message I received?* You may want to ask a friend to do the same thing for you: to listen with their ears, their eyes and their hearts, and then give you feedback regarding the congruency of your message.

Exploring My Understanding

Complete the following sentence: To me, *communicating with my body* means . . .

Considering My Options

Complete the following sentence: NOW I'm going to . . .

RESOLVING CONFLICTS AMICABLY

Conflicts in our relationships—no matter how strong they are—are inevitable. Conflicts arise because we don't always agree with another person's point of view, direction or their ideas, or understand the rationale for their thoughts, feelings and behaviors. Conflict is one of the great spices of life because it reminds us of our humanness and our uniqueness. Rather than automatically conclude that our conflict is unhealthy, remember that out of conflict comes growth opportunities for everyone involved. Being involved in a conflict often forces us to move out of our comfort zones as we consider another's point of view. It often compels us to examine what we think and believe about a situation. It can urge us to look closely at what we say and do to determine if there's a congruency within our selves.

Conflict generally goes unresolved because of barriers we construct to cut off meaningful communication. There are many ways we deal with conflict. The method we use depends on the emotional investment we've made in the situation. We frequently seek out ways to avoid dealing with the disagreement, particularly when we expect our ideas to be rejected. Sometimes we push ahead with what we want without any regard for what others think, need or want. There are times when we will accommodate another's desires rather than taking steps to see that our own are met. We give up satisfying our own needs. Often we see conflict resolution as a lose-lose situation: We both agree to lose something in order to get to a resolution. And a few of us will use conflict as stepping stones for learning more about our selves and another person and for creating new solutions to the conflict.

Every conflict will not be resolved to everyone's satisfaction. We may want others to see our point when they don't and no amount of explaining or reasoning convinces them otherwise. One way to resolve a conflict is to agree to disagree. The most effective way of dealing with conflict is to openly communicate with others.

My Previous Experiences With Resolving Conflicts Amicably

Write down your experiences with resolving conflicts amicably.

My Feelings About These Experiences

Write down your feelings about these experiences.

Suggested Exercise

When you find your self in a conflict situation, use the following process to examine your role, to identify the barriers to resolution, and to determine what proactive steps you can take to resolve the conflict amicably.

STEP 1. Identify the Problem and Ownership.

- I see it this way . . .
- She sees it this way . . .
- The problem belongs to . . .

STEP 2. Identify the Barriers to Communication.

- Preventing me from hearing his point of view is . . .
- Preventing her from hearing my point of view is . . .
- I can improve my communication by . . .
- I can improve my listening by . . .

STEP 3. Identify Possible Solutions.

- Possible solutions include . . .
- The most feasible solution is . . .
- Benefits for me include . . .
- Benefits for him include . . .

STEP 4. Communicate Solutions.

- I will communicate my "best" solution by saying . . .
- She might offer the following objections . . .
- I will respond to the objections by . . .
- I am willing to compromise on the following points . . .

Exploring My Understanding

Complete the following sentence: To me, *resolving conflicts amicably* means . . .

Considering My Options:

Complete the following sentence: NOW I'm going to . . .

COOPERATING CONSCIOUSLY

There is an unstated expectation that we cooperate with others—the people at work, the people in our family and the people in our community. And we do cooperate to a certain extent: We don't purposefully get in somebody else's way. We act as though cooperation means refraining from interference rather than making a real effort to see a project through to completion or to help others get what they want.

If you're reluctant to be cooperative, your reluctance generally has an influence that extends far beyond what's transpiring between you and those you're working with. If others see you as being uncooperative, they too may choose to be uncooperative because of their perception of your status or their relationship with you.

When you put conscious thought into your efforts to complete a task or to help others, you're doing more than just not interfering. You're making a conscious choice about how you can impact that person's ability to make whatever contribution they can make to a project and to get what they want. Cooperating consciously is proactive in nature.

It's reality that you don't always choose to be cooperative. If you aren't willing to assist another person, tell him or her directly rather than saying you'll cooperate when you really mean you won't interfere. You'll find that mutual benefit can be realized when people work together with a common purpose—even if the purpose is not specifically your own.

My Previous Experiences With Cooperating Consciously

Write down your experiences with cooperating consciously.

My Feelings About These Experiences

Write down your feelings about these experiences.

Suggested Exercise

Make a list of people with whom you're expected to cooperate on a regular basis. Using the definition that cooperation is *making a conscious effort to help others get what they want* or *working effectively as a team,* determine to what extent you are truly cooperating. You may want to develop a scale with one being *not at all* and ten being *as much as possible.* For those with whom your cooperation is minimal, determine at least one way you can more consciously cooperate with them. You may want to use this exercise from time to time to assess you cooperativeness with others.

Exploring My Understanding

Complete the following sentence: To me, *cooperating consciously* means . . .

Considering My Options:

Complete the following sentence: Now I'm going to . . .

ENJOYING PHYSICAL TOUCH

Results from numerous research studies support that human beings have a need for the positive nurturing of physical touch from the very beginning of life. Touch connects us with others. Physical nurturing can make the difference between living a connected life and living one of isolation. It can make a difference in how we feel about our selves, how we project our values, talents and skills to others, and how we interact with others. When we make an affirming physical connection with another person, we convey feelings and send messages, and we provide assurance, nurturance, energy and rejuvenation. We convey our feelings of care and love to others. Our skin is a sensor, transmitting messages sent by touch throughout the body.

Touch not only stimulates our feelings, it also stimulates us physiologically. Be selective in your touch. Choose only to touch those with whom you have a relationship. If you're not sure if the other person will appreciate your touching, ask them!

Touching affirms that you're connected to life. Touching often conveys feelings that we possibly can't express with words. Positive touch feels good. The body, mind and spirit benefit, too.

A Special Note: In this exercise, we're discussing affirming nurturing touch. There is no place or purpose for violating touch or for nonconsensual sexual touch. It's never recommended that you impose physical contact onto others. The act of touching is to be reserved for those people with whom you feel a connection and want to confirm that connection with physical closeness. People who are indiscriminately *touchy-feely* with everyone they come into contact with are perceived as insincere. Their actions also create discomfort for those who don't enjoy physical contact with people they don't know well. Their motive for their actions is often suspect, too. Mutual agreement is imperative when engaging in physical touch.

My Previous Experiences With Enjoying Physical Touch

Write down your experiences with enjoying physical touch.

My Feelings About These Experiences

Write down your feelings about these experiences.

Suggested Exercise

Pick a day when you want to monitor how you feel when you're being touched by other people. After each touching encounter, take a few moments to reflect on how you felt during and after the touching. *Did you feel affirmed or did you feel violated? Is this person a person you have a relationship with or one who is casual about his or her touching behavior?*

If your feelings about the experience aren't positive ones, make a commitment to your self to tell the other person that you don't want them touching you. Or tell them under what circumstances you would enjoy being touched. Being direct with your self and another person about touching behavior takes guts and strength. Keep in mind that you're worth it! In every circumstance you want all of the touches you experience to be positive and affirming. Remember, it's *your* body. You have the right and responsibility to interact with people on the level of your choice.

Exploring My Understanding

Complete the following sentence: To me, *enjoying physical touch* means . . .

Considering My Options:

Complete the following sentence: NOW I'm going to . . .

NURTURING A BROAD SUPPORT SYSTEM

Relationships come in all shapes, sizes and levels of intensity. Some of them are very brief, whereas others are everlasting. We need relationships on a number of different levels. We cannot expect everyone we know to be our best friend. Nor can we expect to have a fulfilled life if we maintain only superficial relationships with everyone. It's also important to recognize that relationships come and go—sometimes people who have been your good friends disappear—for reasons that often have nothing to do with you. There's no argument, there's no good-bye, there's no closure to the relationship. Relationships sometimes end because of external circumstances, such as marriage, a change in jobs, the arrival of a baby, pursuit of different interests or a move.

It's beneficial to consider the levels of relationships. Brief contacts are people you meet when you're on a trip, those you see at the cleaners or standing in line at checkout counters. You may never learn their names nor see them again.

Acquaintances are people you know at work, the pharmacist, people in volunteer associations or business groups and people in your neighborhood. You know them by name and greet them when you see them.

Your friends are people with whom you interact socially. You go out to dinner or concerts together. You invite each other over for parties or cookouts. You share commonalities because of where you live, work, or your kids' activities. Whatever commonality you share is the reason for your relationship, often ending when the commonality dissolves.

Your best friends are those people who know just about everything about you, your past and your present, and still care for and love you anyway. They stick with you through the changes you experience in your life as you do with them. They care about you even when they don't agree with what you're doing. You're both heroes and cheerleaders for one another. You share your deepest desires with them. They are there for you *no matter what.*

The relationships that are the rarest are your emotionally intimate relationships. To develop and nurture intimacy with one another, you're compelled to put aside all inhibitions and all barriers to communication. You find safety in exposing your weaknesses, your doubts and your fears. Each of you supports the other's right to and responsibility for continuous growth and development. An intimate relationship is one in which there are no hidden agendas, where openness and directness is the expectation, where feelings are expressed and accepted, and where disagreements are resolved amicably. When you're intimately involved with one another, you're willing to delay gratification of your needs in order to help the other.

We need to nurture a broad support system. We need people at all levels of involvement because different needs can be met, and wants can be satisfied, by different types of relationships.

My Previous Experiences With Nurturing A Broad Support System

Write down your experiences with nurturing a broad support system.

My Feelings About These Experiences

Write down your feelings about these experiences.

Suggested Exercise

Examine your support system. Draw concentric circles on a piece of paper. Label the innermost circle "Intimate Friends." Label the next circle "Best Friends." Label the next one "Friends" and the next one "Acquaintances." Then label the outermost circle "Brief Contacts." Next, think about each of your relationships. Write those names in the appropriate circles. Pay careful attention to those persons with whom you share an intimate relationship—where you're the most honest with your self and with that person, where you feel the most vulnerable. After examining your relationships, think about what you might like to do to strengthen your support system.

Exploring My Understanding

Complete the following sentence: To me, *nurturing a broad support system* means . . .

Considering My Options

Complete the following sentence: NOW I'm going to . . .

LAUGHING ABOUT MY SELF AND LIFE

It seems that the more serious we take life on a daily basis, the more uncomfortable we feel about our selves. We often have difficulty determining what's really important and what's trivial. In the grand scheme of things, those that are important significantly impact the lives of people. The incidents that result in mere inconveniences are not.

None of us like to be laughed at because of our mistakes or poor judgment (as defined by someone else). Many of us have been humiliated for attempting a task and falling flat on our faces because we didn't have all the information we needed in order to complete the task more accurately. Some of us have been the victims of circumstances when others have even withheld information so we'd look ridiculous.

It's really up to you to decide how serious a situation really is and what action needs to be taken. Keep in mind that the more emotionally involved you are in a situation, the more serious you consider it to be. Sometimes things seem very serious when they're occurring. When the urgency or danger of the situation has passed, then we can find humor in our actions or those of others. In the big scheme of things, how serious is it that you parked your car in a parking lot while you went off with friends to come back and find that the gates to the parking lot had been locked? Frustrating, yes! Inconvenient, yes! Possibly embarrassing, yes! Serious, No!

Take another situation that's serious: driving too fast for road conditions, requiring you to swerve in order to miss an oncoming car. Not only could you have been seriously injured or killed, so could the driver and passengers in the other cars.

Both of these incidences involved cars, people and perhaps, poor judgment. The impact on people differs. The consequences of having your car locked in a parking lot is far from earth-shattering. The consequences of driving too fast for the prevailing conditions could be devastating. So when you're looking at your self and life, laugh at those times when you or others were merely inconvenienced or you didn't use your best judgment. Save your serious side for those times when people's lives can be negatively impacted.

My Previous Experiences With Laughing About My Self And Life

Write down your experiences with laughing at your self and life.

My Feelings About These Experiences

Write down your feelings about these experiences.

Suggested Exercises

1. When you find that you're taking your self and life too seriously, ask your self these questions: *In the big scheme of things, will this incident matter in ten years? Am I merely being inconvenienced? Will the outcome of this situation impact me or the lives of others?*

2. Make a list of ten incidents where you made a mistake or goofed. You'll enjoy telling these stories and others will enjoy hearing them. This is a great way to celebrate your humanness.

Exploring My Understanding

Complete the following sentence: To me, *laughing about my self and life* means . . .

Considering My Options

Complete the following sentence: NOW I'm going to . . .

ENJOYING LIFE

When we are born, there is no guarantee about the length of time we will live our lives. We really don't know from one moment to the next if this one will be our last. Given this reality, doesn't it make sense to enjoy living each moment to its fullest rather than waiting for "some day" or retirement? So many people work hard all of their lives with the goal of enjoying life when they retire. We really don't know if we'll ever reach retirement. We may spend much of our lives working, foregoing the enjoyable and never experience the goal. Work is important, and so is pleasure. When we enjoy what we're doing, whether it's work or fun, we have a greater sense about the meaning of life and our place in it. We are more fully integrated when we combine work with pleasure, and *doing* with *being*.

My Previous Experiences With Enjoying Life

Write down your experiences with enjoying life.

My Feelings About These Experiences

Write down your feelings about these experiences.

Suggested Exercise

Using visual representation, such as pictures, words, or symbols, identify those activities you enjoy doing. Note the last time you enjoyed each activity. Look at the activities you identified again. Select at least one and make a plan to engage in that activity this week. Each week add another activity until enjoying life is part of your routine rather than something you're putting off until *one of these days.*

Exploring My Understanding

Complete the following sentence: To me, *enjoying life* means . . .

Considering My Options

Complete the following sentence: NOW I'm going to . . .

SEEING THE WORLD THROUGH ANOTHER'S
POINT OF VIEW

No two of us see the world exactly alike. Our vision is colored by experiences, biases, values, prejudices and aspirations. Just because we have unique perspectives doesn't excuse us from seeking to understand how another views the world.

Think about the survivor of the World War II Holocaust—how would he view the world? Or what about the Southeast Asian refugee who was a medical doctor in her country and now runs a dry cleaners in the U.S.? How about the child from the inner city project who witnesses crimes right in front of his eyes daily? Or have you considered how a blind person views a world that she's possibly never actually seen? Or take someone who's serving time for a crime he's committed, what's his view of the world? How about an elderly relative who's witnessed wars and changes in society and lifestyles?

Every one of us brings something different to our understanding of the world. When we endeavor to look at the world from another's point of view, we learn many things. We learn there's more than one way to look at every situation. We learn that challenges come in varying degrees with varying levels of intensity. We learn that the human spirit is strong and enduring. We learn more about our own values and biases. We learn more about others. We learn how we can more effectively communicate with one another. Seeing the world through another's point of view will broaden our awareness and deepen our understanding.

My Previous Experiences With Seeing The World From Another's Point Of View

Write down your experiences with seeing the world through another's point of view.

My Feelings About These Experiences

Write down your feelings about these experiences.

Suggested Exercise

Invite someone you feel has had a number of experiences different from your own to spend an hour or two with you for a picnic or a nature walk or any other activity that is conducive to talking and sharing with one another. Ask questions about his or her viewpoint regarding a wide variety of topics. Listen very carefully to what is said. Ask questions if you need clarification. Make every effort to put your self in their place so you can have some empathy with their experiences and their view of the world. Share your point of view if you're asked. Keep in mind the purpose of your discussion. Thank the person for his or her help in the process of your growth and understanding. You can use this inquiry method any time you have an opportunity to talk with others.

Exploring My Understanding

Complete the following sentence: To me, *seeing the world from another's point of view* means . . .

Considering My Options

Complete the following sentence: NOW I'm going to . . .

PART THREE

MOVING ON!

9
Strategies for Living InSync

Accept your humanness.
Develop a clear vision.
Love your self unconditionally.
Express your self.
Stretch your mental capacity.
Take risks.
Nurture your relationships.
Rest and relax your body.
Exercise regularly.
Eat nutritiously.

If living *InSync* appeals to you, here are some ideas to keep in mind. Remember that living *InSync* is a *process* that continuously demands that you grow, stretch and move out of your comfort zone. Keep these strategies handy so they'll serve as a gentle reminder. Post them in places you frequent.

1. Accept your humanness. Humanness means imperfection—making mistakes. Ask your self how you can profit from the mistakes you make. Will you celebrate them? How can you profit from your successes? Accept the humanness of others, too.

Remember to forgive your self and others for making mistakes. Dynamic energy is released through forgiveness. With freedom, you can channel your energy into productive endeavors.

2. Have a clear vision. Know what it is you want and nurture that crystal clear vision. Keep what you want to do with your life foremost in your mind's eye. Set goals for reaching desired professional aspirations, desired levels of achievement or desired personal accomplishments.

Whether you want to be the CEO, the most recognized professional in your field or a parent, remember that setting and pursuing your goals will enable YOU to get what YOU want. Use your goals for planning and prioritizing your daily, weekly, monthly and annual activities. Stay in touch with what you want so you can maximize the use of your time, energy and resources.

3. Love your self unconditionally. This is a tough one, isn't it? Accept your self just as you are right now. Feel deep unrelenting love for your self as a human being. Constantly recall you're unique and worthy.

Refrain from waiting until you've made some major change in your self before you feel you deserve your own love. Keep in mind that it's hard for others to love us when we don't love our selves. Loving your self just as you are means that no matter where you are in your development, you are a valuable human being.

4. Express your self. As you live *InSync*, you have much to express. Feel comfortable with your feelings, ideas and opinions. It's your right to think and feel any way you think and feel. Let your desires and needs be known to those people who can help you. Look for creative ways to express your self. Remember your expression is a reflection of your self—a different and unique way of interacting with your world. Provide outlets for emotive and creative expression.

5. Stretch your mental capacity. Learn how to do something new. Be eager to take a risk! Look for learning opportunities and creative ways to handle life's challenges. Remember you can learn how to do anything you want. It's a matter of investing your time, energy and resources into the learning process.

Are you still curious about what makes life tick? Have you sought answers to those questions that have intrigued you for a long time? Are you a student of life? Are you now looking at your world differently than you did six months ago? Move out of your comfort zone—get out of that proverbial rut of "sameness."

6. Take risks. Be willing to experience the unknown! Be open to the many possibilities life has to offer. Be eager to experience life as a new adventure on a daily basis. Remember that taking the risk—experiencing the unknown and the unpredictable—is important!

Without risk and without moving out of your comfort zone, you miss many opportunities to grow and expand your horizons. You can overcome fear. You can make changes in a situation that doesn't currently suit you. You must be willing to ACT. You must be willing to invest your time, energy and resources. Old methods for experiencing life will tend to yield the same results.

7. Nurture your relationships. Offer support and encouragement to others so they can help them selves find their own ways. Spend time with your loved ones. Take care of those routine matters AND enjoy laughing, playing and having fun. Really listen to what others have to say. Resolve conflicts amicably whenever possible. Recognize that differences in people do exist, that everyone doesn't see things the way you do and that these differences are healthy.

8. Rest and relax your body. Remember to treat your body with respect. It is the present home for your mind and soul. Avoid illness and injury by finding ways to relax each day. Give your body adequate time for rest and sleep. Respond to your body's request for additional rest when you're feeling more stressed than usual.

9. Exercise regularly. Exercise regularly for increased aerobic capacity, flexibility, strength and endurance. Set up a routine so you work out three to four times a week. Pick exercises you enjoy. Develop a system that works for you.

10. Eat nutritiously. Remember to maintain your body by eating a variety of healthy foods. Make conscious choices about what and when you eat. Limit your intake of foods and additives, such as sugar, alcohol and caffeine, that are known to have debilitating effects on your body.

10
Making a Lifetime Commitment

A PROCESS

Living InSync will render all of your heart's desires. Investing in your self is the most important action you can ever take. What you do with your time, energy and resources is entirely up to you. You have choices to make. Make choices that work for you. Just like life, love, success and happiness, living InSync is a process. The day does not come when you've arrived and can sit back in your easy chair and rest. Life is dynamic and ever changing. If you choose not to move along with it, opportunities to enjoy life's enriching experiences will pass you by. When you're in the process of living InSync, you don't want to miss anything. You want to experience all life has to offer.

So in the long run, reaching the goal of living InSync is really irrelevant. Being in the process of living InSync is the essence of life. The *process* is fundamental.

A COMMITMENT

The good that comes to you in life comes as a result of the commitment you make to your self to be and do your best. Your best becomes better each day because you're expanding your horizons through the exploration of your thoughts, feelings and experiences.

Renewing the commitment to be your best on a daily basis is important. Otherwise you may become lazy and out of focus. You may lose your vision. Commitment energizes your abilities. Committing to be your best at every moment and doing your best in every action, based on what you know and feel, is a difficult choice. This choice is essential—for then you are compelled to find the meaning in your life on a daily basis.

Commitment means you don't give up when situations aren't as you'd like them to be. It means you press onward even when you can't clearly see your way. It means you push pass the fears that would inhibit you from being your best.

CHALLENGE AND GROWTH

Once the growth process has begun, it's hard to stop it or put it on hold. Your subconscious mind continually looks for new growth opportunities. These opportunities often come in simple forms, such as really seeing a flower in the garden for the first time or reading a poem or listening to the wisdom of a mentor. With every challenge you face, you grow—spiritually, emotionally, mentally, physically and socially. Your challenges prepare you for the next step in your development—for the next challenge. When the challenge seems overwhelming, take a few moments to reflect on other challenges you've conquered.

Know that you have the power within your self to do whatever it is you want to do or are required to do by life's circumstances. Your challenges compel you to live InSync and to solidly connect you to your spiritual dimension.

MOVE OUT OF YOUR COMFORT ZONE

When you make a lifetime investment in your self, you're pledging your willingness to move out of your comfort zone. Your comfort zone is often narrow in scope so you don't really have to move that far to move into a new experience.

The movement might come when you try a new food for the first time or tell another person how you really feel about them, or when you listen even though you'd rather talk. Your comfort zone is the status quo, habits, values, thoughts, biases, prejudices and traditions. Adding diversions to your daily experiences propels you into new experiences.

TAKE RISKS

By merely being involved in living InSync, you're taking a risk. The commitment you make to your self will likely draw criticism from those who know you—those you're connected to through various relationships.

Others often don't understand your need to be in control of your life. They take your movement along a different path as being a criticism of the way they live their lives. They often feel rejected, left behind or angry because your behavior differs from their expectations. Then there are those who support and encourage you as you move through life in your own style.

By pursuing life InSync, you take a risk because you don't always know who will support and encourage you. There are times when the intensity of a relationship fades out because of your need to take yet another risk—to experience life from yet another perspective. The advantages of taking risks significantly outweigh the disadvantages.

EXERCISE *GENTLE* CONTROL

Maintaining a balance between rigid control and a lack-adaisical approach to being responsible for your life is challenging. Rigid control is full of *shoulds* and *oughts* that constantly remind us that everything isn't perfect. Whatever will be will be is the slogan of the lackadaisical approach—relinquishing your responsibility for your life.

When you exercise *gentle* control, you're purpose-driven, goal-directed and open to opportunities that come your way. You're willing to look at each opportunity to determine if taking advantage of it will move you closer to reaching your goals. *Gentle* control implies flexibility. The more flexible you are, the more you trust your self to take what's good and beneficial out of life.

BE GENTLE WITH YOUR SELF

Any time you start a new project, you want everything to be perfect—circumstances, the behavior of others, and your own meticulous planning and implementation of your plan. If, on some unpredictable day, your choices are not the best ones for you, what good does it do to beat your self up? Recognize that no matter how precisely you make your plan, there will be days that you're going to "fall off the wagon." When this happens, get up, reconfirm your commitment to your self, and move forward. Look at the reason you've slipped, store that information for future use, and move on. Look at the lesson you've learned from the experience. Be gentle with your self as you unfold and become the best you can be. Celebrate your humanness.

USE YOUR RESOURCES

Resources come in many shapes, sizes and configurations. Resources may include money, investments, property, research, printed and spoken words, other people and always your self. You have within your self all you need to know to move ahead in your life. You have within your self the power to do whatever it is you need and want to do. Every time you invest in your self, you're investing in others as well.

Put aside your reluctance to use your "other people" resource. Dismiss your need to be proud, your concerns about what they'll think, your embarrassment and your sense of self-sufficiency. Be willing to be vulnerable. If you let any of your fears stop you from maximizing the use of your "other people" resource, you'll inhibit your own growth and development. You can learn so much from others if you're willing to take the risk and if you'll listen. Keep in mind that the most valuable of all resources have nothing to do with money and possessions.

SHARE YOUR EXPERIENCES

As you move through the process of living InSync with life and your self, you learn much. You'll be learning how you can invest in your life and move out of your comfort zone. You'll learn how you can get everything you want out of life, how you can truly realize the goals you've set for your self. You'll learn how you can maximize the use of your time, energy, and resources. When you invest in your self, you have so much more to share with others. The more you grow, the more you'll feel compelled to support others in their growth and development. Through your words and actions, encourage them to set out on their own journey—to engage in the process of living InSync—of creating the life they want for them selves. Encourage them to find the joy that comes from being in *gentle* control of life. Sharing with others is your responsibility.

Epilogue

*By adapting the practical philosophy of Living InSync,
you have unequivocal access to your Personal Power.*

*When You Live InSync,
The Outcome Of Every Thought,
Word, Emotion And Action Is…*

*Coexistent
Compatible
Concurrent
Congruent
Consistent
Cooperative
Harmonious
Simultaneous
and
Unified.*

Suggested Readings & Listenings

TO EXPAND YOUR AWARENESS AND INCREASE YOUR KNOWLEDGE ABOUT THE DIMENSIONS, EXPLORE THESE RESOURCES:

Growing InSync with the Spiritual Dimension

Back, R. (1970). *Jonathan Livingston Seagull*. New York: Avon.

Bradshaw, J. (1990). *Homecoming: Reclaiming and Championing Your Inner Child*. New York: Bantam.

Chopra, D. (1992). *The Higher Self*. (Cassette Recording Audiocassette No. 255). Chicago: Nightingale-Conant.

Chopra D. (1992). *Unconditional Life*. New York: Harmony.

Dyer, W. W. (1985). *Choosing Your Own Greatness*. (Cassette Recording Audiocassette No. 853). Chicago: Nightingale-Conant.

Johnson, S. (1985). *One Minute for Myself*. New York: William Morrow.

Paulus, T. (1972). *Hope for the Flowers*. New York: Paulist Press.

Peck, M. S. (1978). *The Road Less Traveled*. New York: Simon & Schuster.

Pilgrim, M. S. (1991). *The Seashore Collection*. (Cassette Recording Audiocassette). Atlanta: Life Investments.

Waitley, D.E. (1987). *Being the Best*. New York: Pocket Books.

Growing InSync with the Emotional Dimension

Borysenko, J. (1990). *Guilt Is the Teacher, Love Is the Lesson.* New York: Warner.

Bradshaw, J. (1988). *Healing The Shame That Binds You.* Deerfield Beach, FL: Health Communications.

Jampolsky, G. G. (1979). *Love is Letting Go of Fear.* Celestial Arts.

Johnson, S. (1985). *One Minute for Myself.* New York: William Morrow.

Miller, A. (1981). *The Drama of the Gifted Child.* New York: Basic.

Parker, J. (1986). *Coping with Emotions.* (Cassette Recording Audiocassette). Ojai, CA: Jonathan Parker's Gateways Institute.

Paulus, T. (1972). *Hope for the Flowers.* New York: Paulist Press.

Peale, N. V. (1987). *The Power of Positive Thinking.* (Cassette Recording Audiocassette No. 427). Chicago: Nightingale-Conant.

Pilgrim. M. S. (1991, November). Dealing with Disappointment. *Atlanta Health And Fitness Magazine.*

Pilgrim. M. S. (1991). *The Seashore Collection.* (Cassette Recordings Audiocassette). Atlanta: Life Investments.

Pilgrim. M. S. (1991, February) Talking to Yourself? Make It Positive. *Atlanta Health And Fitness Magazine.*

Piper, W. (1974) *The Little Engine that Could.* New York: Platt & Munk.

Thomas, M.; Steinmen, G. & Pogregin, L. C. (1974). *Free to Be . . . You and Me.* New York: McGraw-Hill.

Growing InSync with the Mental Dimension

Bliss, E. C. *Doing It Now.* (Cassette Recording Audiocassette No. 1031). Chicago: Nightingale-Conant.

Culligan, M. J. & Sedlacek, K. (1980). *How to Avoid Stress Before It Kills You.* New York: Gramercy.

Davis, M.; Eshelman, E. R. & McKay, M. (1988). *The Relaxation And Stress Reduction Workbook.* Oakland, CA: New Harbinger.

Eliot, R. S. & Breo, D. L. (1984). *Is It Worth Dying For*. New York: Bantam.

Herrmann, N. (1989). *The Creative Brain*. Lake Lure, NC: Brain Books.

LeBoeuf, M. (1987). *Working Smarter*. (Cassette Recording Audiocassette No. 170). Chicago: Nightingale-Conant.

Pilgrim, M.S. (1991, January). Setting Goals: How to Get What You Want. *Atlanta Health And Fitness Magazine*.

Pilgrim, M.S. (1991, April). What's Important to You? You Can Make It Happen. *Atlanta Health And Fitness Magazine*.

Pilgrim, M.S. (1992, June). The Decision Dilemma. *Atlanta Health And Fitness Magazine*.

Rose, C. (1985). *Accelerated Learning*. New York: Dell.

Scott, D. (1980). *How to Put More Time in Your Life*. New York: Rawson, Wade.

von Oech, R. (1984). *A Whack on the Side of the Head*. New York: Warner Brothers.

von Oech, R. (1987). *How You Can Be More Creative*. (Audiocassette Recording No. 438). Chicago: Nightingale-Conant.

Ziglar, Z. *Goals: How to Set Them, How to Reach Them*. (Cassette Recording Audiocassette No. 483). Chicago: Nightingale-Conant.

Growing InSync with the Physical Dimension

Benson, H. (1975). *The Relaxation Response*. New York: William Morrow.

Brody, J. (1987). *Jane Brody's Good Food Book*. New York: Bantam.

Brody, J. (1987). *Jane Brody's Nutrition Book*. New York: Bantam.

Colbin, A. (1986). *Food and Healing*. New York: Ballantine.

Cooper, K. (1982). *The Aerobics Program for Total Well-Being: Exercise, Diet, Emotional Balance*. New York: M. Evans.

Davis, M., Eshelman, E.R. & McKay, M. (1988). *The Relaxation and Stress Reduction Workbook*. Oakland, CA: New Harbinger.

Hittleman, R. (1969). *Yoga: 28 Day Exercise Plan*. New York: Bantam.

Pilgrim, M.S. (1991). *The Seashore Collection*. (Audiocassette Recordings.) Atlanta: Life Investments.

Portugues, G. & Vedral, J. L. (1988). *Hard Bodies Express Workout*. New York: Dell.

Robertson, L.; Flinders, C. & Ruppenthal, B. (1986). *The New Laurel's Kitchen*. Berkely, CA: Ten Speed.

Wardell, J. (1986). *Thin Within: How to Eat and Live Like a Thin Person*. New York: Pocket Books.

Growing InSync with the Social Dimension

Arapakis, M. (1987). *How to Speak Up, Set Limits and Say No*. (Cassette Recording Audiocassette). Boulder: CareerTrack.

Buscaglia, L. F. *Loving Each Other: The Challenge of Human Relationships*. Thorofare, NJ: SLACK.

Lobel, A. (1972). *Frog and Toad Together*. New York: Harper & Row.

Pease, A. (1984). *Signals: How to Use Body Language for Power, Success and Love*. New York: Bantam.

Pilgrim, M. S. (1991, June). How to Fight Fair: Resolving Conflicts in Relationships. *Atlanta Health and Fitness Magazine*.

Quebin, N. (1988). *How to Be a Great Communicator: In Person, on Paper and on the Podium*. (Cassette Recording Audiocassette No. 472). Chicago: Nightingale-Conant.

Smith, M. J. (1975). *When I Say No, I Feel Guilty*. New York: Bantam.

Solomon, L.U. (1985). *The Friendship of Hesper and Rani*. Fort Bragg, CA: Mendocino Lithograph.

Sparks, A. H. (1979). *Hope for the Frogs*. Sacramento: Jalmar.

Tannen, D. (1990). *You Just Don't Understand*. New York: Ballantine.

For a comprehensive list of references and works by the author, contact Life Investments by calling (800) 730-0662 or (404) 432-7100.

About the Author

Susan Pilgrim, Ph.D., president of Life Investments, is an Atlanta-based international speaker and consultant. She's committed to positively influencing the lives of those with whom she crosses paths. "Take *gentle* control of your life" is one of the powerful principles of living InSync that she shares with her audiences. She encourages all who experience her work to invest in themselves so they can get what they want in life. Her thought-provoking messages have inspired many listeners to move out of their comfort zones. Many have acknowledged her gift for touching people's lives.

Susan's work represents a unique blend of experience and education in the areas of business management, education and psychology. Corporations, associations, government agencies and educational institutions benefit from the programs she designs to specifically address their objectives. Her regular columns are featured in a number of health, personal development and business publications.

Customized workshops, keynotes, seminars and consulting services in the following areas are available from Life Investments:

- Change Management
- Conflict Resolution
- Enhancing Performance
- Living InSync
- Stress Management

- Communication Skills
- Empowerment
- Goal Setting
- Self-Esteem
- Team Building

If you're interested in knowing more about Susan's work or want to discuss a possible workshop or speaking engagement, contact her by calling 1-800-730-0662 or (404) 432-7100.